I CAN LEARN WHEN I'M MOVING

Going to School with ADHD

NICOLE BISCOTTI, M.ED.
WITH HELP FROM HER SON, JASON

WHAT EDUCATORS, PARENTS, & ADHD ADVOCATES HAVE TO SAY ABOUT THIS BOOK

"It is so important that this book is read by both parents and teachers. Nicole's honesty and realistic commitment to students with ADHD leaps off every page. I have read many books on education and ADHD, rarely do you hear the voice of a young person with ADHD whose viewpoint is explored at such length and with evident self-perception and placed alongside continual discussion of educational theory and practice."

— TONY LLOYD, CHIEF EXECUTIVE, ADHD FOUNDATION NEURODIVERSITY CHARITY

"This should be required reading for every teacher! The book contains many stories, strategies, and concepts that are so important for us to know about when supporting a student with ADHD. My only regret is that it wasn't written when I was a child/teen who was struggling with ADHD and nobody knew about it or how to support and encourage me. Nicole does a fine job presenting information as both an educator and as a parent. You definitely should go out and get this book today!"

— DR. BRYAN PEARLMAN, EDD, LMSW, FOUNDER & HEAD TRAINER OF MOST VALUABLE PROFESSIONAL DEVELOPMENT

"Nicole and Jason have provided readers with a unique perspective, one that is only experienced by those on the journey, and each educator inspired to give every child what they most need has the opportunity to benefit profoundly from Nicole and Jason's journey. For it is the child's perspective that is often overlooked, even ignored, during their educational experience and within most (IEP/504) meetings. As a neurotypical parent of a bright dyslexic-ADHD child, I wish Nicole and Jason's perspectives were available when we were struggling through the public education system K-3. This book is exceptional as are ADHD's exceptionalities, and I'm honored to know Nicole."

— MARILYN MULLER, MOM, FOUNDER OF MOM'S FOR FREE APPROPRIATE PUBLIC-FUNDED EDUCATION (#MOMS4FAPE)

"Every now and then a book comes out that is a 'must' for educators and parents to read. Nicole Biscotti, a teacher, collaborates with her son, Jason, on what it means to go to school with ADHD. Each chapter opens with Jason's perspective and Nicole's insights to spark conversations to better support children with ADHD. *I Can Learn When I'm Moving* is what we need now: a mother/son team sharing authentic experiences along with stories, research, strategies, and a toolbox for ADHD accommodations."

— BARBARA BRAY, EDUCATOR, COACH, SPEAKER, PODCAST HOST, AUTHOR OF DEFINE YOUR WHY

Copyright © 2021 by Nicole Biscotti, M.Ed.
Published by EduMatch®
PO Box 150324, Alexandria, VA 22315
www.edumatchpublishing.com

All rights reserved. No portion of this book may be reproduced in any form without permission from the publisher, except as permitted by U.S. copyright law. For permissions contact sarah@edumatch.org.

These books are available at special discounts when purchased in quantities of 10 or more for use as premiums, promotions fundraising, and educational use. For inquiries and details, contact the publisher: sarah@edumatch.org.

ISBN: 978-1-953852-10-6

CONTENTS

A.D.H.D	vii
Author's Note	xiii
Introduction	xvii
1. A Population at Risk: Suspended, Kicked Out, & Expelled...All Before First Grade	1
2. ADHD in the Classroom: The Many Faces of ADHD	15
3. "Maybe He's Possessed?" Addressing the ADHD Gap in Teacher Education	39
4. Relationships - Opportunities for Impact	57
5. ADHDers Raise the Bar for Everyone	73
6. Whole-Class Strategies that Address the Needs of Children with ADHD	89
7. Teacher's Toolbox: Subject Specific ADHD Accommodations for All	103
8. I NEED to move! — Living with Hyperactivity	119
9. Making Friends - Supporting ALL Students in Inclusion	129
10. The ADHD Village	145
Let's bring the #ADHDGlobalConvo to your school!	155
References	157
Contributing Authors	165
About the Author	167
My Story of WHY I Became a Teacher	169

A.D.H.D

Author Unknown

*Take my hand and **come with me**,*
I want to teach you about ADHD.
I need you to know, I want to explain,
I have a very different brain.
Sights, sounds, and thoughts collide.
What to do first? I can't decide.
Please understand I'm not to blame,
I just can't process things the same.

*Take my hand and **walk with me**,*
Let me show you about ADHD.
I try to behave, I want to be good,
But I sometimes forget to do as I should.
Walk with me and wear my shoes,

You'll see it's not the way I'd choose.
I do know what I'm supposed to do,
But my brain is slow getting the message through.

*Take my hand and **talk with me**,*
I want to tell you about ADHD.
I rarely think before I talk,
I often run when I should walk.
It's hard to get my school work done,
My thoughts are outside having fun.
I never know just where to start,
I think with my feelings and see with my heart.

*Take my hand and **stand by me**,*
I need you to know about ADHD.
It's hard to explain but thought you to know,
I can't help letting my feelings show.
Sometimes I'm angry, jealous, or sad.
I feel overwhelmed, frustrated, and mad.
I can't concentrate and I lose all my stuff.
I try really hard but it's never enough.

*Take my hand and **learn with me**,*
We need to know more about ADHD.
I worry a lot about getting things wrong,
Everything I do takes twice as long.
Every day is exhausting for me...
Looking through the fog of ADHD.
I'm often so misunderstood,
I would change in a heartbeat if I could.

*Take my hand and **listen to me**,*
I want to share a secret about ADHD.
I want you to know there is more to me.
I'm not defined by it, you see.
I'm sensitive, kind and lots of fun.
I'm blamed for things I haven't done.
I'm the loyalist friend you'll ever know,
I just need a chance to let it show.

*Take my hand and **look at me**,*
Just forget about the ADHD.
I have real feelings just like you.
The love in my heart is just as true.
I may have a brain that can never rest,
But please understand I'm trying my best.
I want you to know, I need you to see,
I'm more than the label, I am still me!!!!

DEDICATION

This book is for all of the children who are struggling with a myriad of thoughts, impulses, and emotions that they may not even understand, much less be able to express. Children with ADHD have wonderful gifts and unique strengths that are waiting to be developed and encouraged.

This book is also dedicated to the teachers who work with these children each and every day. I honor your willingness to care for other people's children enough to seek to understand.

AUTHOR'S NOTE

Jason and I have worked closely on his contributions to this book. He is a very articulate child, and I have been very careful to tell his stories in his words. He uses the microphone feature instead of typing. He tends to speak in run-on sentences, but I leave all of that because when I read it, I can hear Jason speaking in my head, and that is what I want for you, the reader— *to hear Jason just as he speaks.*

Writing this book together has been an amazing process of increased understanding and healing for both of us. We have discussed in great detail the effects that we hope that our sharing with parents and educators in this book will have on other children. Jason approves every section of this book. We have reviewed everything together, and I've explained all of the "big words." Through the entire writing of this book, Jason has been very clear not only about changes he'd like to see, but also about his choice to continue this project. His enthusiasm for and the pride he takes in writing this book is inspiring to me. Throughout the process of writing this book, Jason had only one condition— that his older twin sisters did not know about our project (they've already found out).

The intention behind sharing Jason's story is primarily to spark conversations that can help us to better support children with ADHD. All insights shared are from the perspective of a child with ADHD, a mother, and a teacher. It is important to note that I am not a trained medical professional, nor am I certified in Special Education. I am a certified secondary Spanish Teacher and hold a Master's Degree in Secondary Education. At the printing of this book, I am completing another Master's Degree in Education Administration. I've also finished about a third of the coursework toward a doctoral degree in Education Leadership. This book should not be used to diagnose anyone or generalize how all children with ADHD should be accommodated at school; it is much more of a reflection, a shared perspective, and a toolbox, than a guide.

CONTRIBUTORS

I could not have offered innovative, researched-based strategies for all learners that accommodate ADHD learners without the contributions of several generous educators. They are experts in their fields, and I encourage you to explore their work. There is information about how you can connect with them and their work at the end of the book. I have learned from each and every one of them on my journey as a mother and teacher of children with ADHD. I'm honored to include their insights in this book.

HOW WILL THIS BOOK HELP YOU?

This book will give you knowledge and perspective that will impact how you approach the education of students with ADHD. You will have research-based, kid-approved strategies for immediate implementation in your classroom or to suggest for your child's learning. You will also gain insight into what it feels like to have ADHD when you're a child and read firsthand accounts from a parent's perspective. This book attempts to close some of the gaps in most teacher education by providing you with practical knowledge about ADHD and whole-class interventions that address the needs of the ADHD learner.

HOW TO USE THIS BOOK

My hope is that educators enjoy reading this book on a quiet evening with their beverage of choice. There are stories here that will make you laugh and maybe even tear up a little as you read about our experiences and reflect on your own. But…I know parents and educators are really busy, like crazy busy sometimes…so I have designed this book so that you can find what you need quickly by topic. Writing the book in this way necessitated some repetition, but I tried to keep that to a minimum so that the book can be enjoyed from cover to cover.

INTRODUCTION

"I want teachers to understand that little kids with ADHD are like good people but they just don't know what to do when they feel angry or bored —sometimes they need an area just to calm down and that's quiet."

Jason, like all children, tells us very clearly what he needs from educators. Sometimes children communicate verbally, and at other times, it's through their behavior. In either case, we must be willing to put down our biases, filters, and assumptions and become present to their needs. Writing about my son's experiences with ADHD has been very healing for both of us. I just apologized to him for not understanding his behavior initially, to which he responded that he wouldn't have known what to do either in my place.

"If I had a kid like me I wouldn't even know what to do with them if they acted so bad. I like writing stories with you mom because I feel like I can open up to myself. The questions you ask are like a challenge and I'm opening up to myself at the same time. It helps me to understand myself more than I do right now."

Mothering a child with ADHD is not for the faint of heart. I have felt ashamed, terrified, confused, lost, and intimidated by teachers, daycare workers, administrators, and counselors many times. This has not been an easy road, and as all parents know;— there is simply nothing harder on this earth than watching your child suffer and not knowing how to help them. I am a teacher, I am highly educated in *education*, and often I do not know what to do.

My heart breaks because I know the kind, empathetic, sensitive little boy with dimples whose self-esteem took a major hit every time he "disappointed me" when I received (yet another) call from the school. Usually, I listened to an administrator, or teacher, or daycare worker who expressed varying degrees of frustration at Jason's behavior, and in those moments, I have felt embarrassed and powerless. The truth is I couldn't make Jason stop throwing things, hitting people, or running away either. Most of the time, as they described the horrible things that Jason had done that day, I just felt sadness because I could only imagine how upset Jason himself was.

You see, it's hard for people to understand that your four-year-old that just attacked a daycare worker is more scared and upset inside than that adult might ever be able to fully know. People, even well-intentioned people, only have so much tolerance for negative behavior. Very few will go beyond the chaos of his actions to begin to understand the "why," much less have the sympathy that a parent's heart does.

In writing this book with Jason, I am not only extending a hand to all of the teachers that are struggling with the challenging behaviors caused by ADHD, but I am also standing up for Jason. I want the child who was acting out so terribly that he had to be put into a restraint —but melted in my arms the minute I arrived at school— to have a voice. As an educator, I cannot shut my eyes to how many

"Jasons" exist in our society. My son is not the only child suffering with ADHD and the list of other conditions that generally come with it, such as Oppositional Disorder, Learning Disability, Anxiety, and Depression.

Many children are struggling, and they are desperately in need of our help. The ADHD population is at risk and is growing. People often comment that when they were younger, they never heard of ADHD, but now "everyone" seems to have it. This has become society's problem or stated another way, ADHD is arguably an issue all know of or have had to deal with personally on different levels.

To help someone, you must first understand their perspective and be able to empathize with them. We have to begin to look past the challenging, even violent behavior, to understand the function or "The WHY." Only then can we begin to address the very real needs of the child. These children will not sit down, be quiet, and listen because they are told to. If you have a child with ADHD, have taught a child with ADHD, or have spent any time with one, you are probably very clear about this. These kids have complex needs and thinking patterns, which are usually coupled with an abundance of energy. We have to dig deeper and expand our own understanding to reach them.

Once we begin to understand the child with ADHD that we love and care for, our work has only just begun. There are no IEPs and 504s in the real world. People can be unkind and unaccepting, and not everyone will want to understand, help, and offer accommodations, especially for those that need them the most. Children with ADHD not only need a caring adult that advocates for them while they are small, but as well they need to be taught additional life and coping skills to be successful in life. I wish I could, but I am not always going to be there to do breathing exercises, offer alternatives to expressing anger, or stop everything to help Jason work through his angry moments that can quickly become violent. Most employers, friends, and potential girlfriends are just not going to tolerate his behavior. That is the bottom line.

Rather than focusing on managing the challenging behavior, we need to look past our reactions and begin to wonder WHY. All of this work begins with an open mind, and an even more open heart. Before we delve into classroom strategies, we must first seek to understand. Much information is to be gained by simply observing and being present. All behavior is communication. Every child is unique, and ADHD presents itself in countless ways.

This is Jason's story, and I hope you learn from it, but the child with ADHD in your classroom has a whole different set of needs waiting to be understood...

A POPULATION AT RISK: SUSPENDED, KICKED OUT, & EXPELLED...ALL BEFORE FIRST GRADE

POINTS TO PONDER

- What is ADHD?
- Why do so many kids seem to have it?
- What are the risks associated? How are kids with ADHD served in schools?
- How does ADHD affect everyone in society?

"*When I was little I got kicked out of a school and I think it was kind of my fault because I did a lot of bad things but kind of not totally my fault because they didn't know how to basically deal with me. The more bad that I was the more they just kept punishing me and it made me feel like I was a bad person. That would just make me feel more upset and then I would just feel like I couldn't control myself more and then they would keep punishing me on and*

on. They just kept putting pressure on me and I just kept getting more out of control myself so I didn't know what to do. I think they felt like I was a bad person and I just kept getting more mad. My feelings were hurt. I used to like to run around because I had so much energy and the person would get super mad so I would run away from them and one time they chased me in the office so I jumped up on the table because I didn't know where else to go. They tried to get me down and I just wanted to get away from them and I kicked them. I got into a lot of trouble but I was just trying to get away from them."

We usually suspend and expel the kids that desperately need to feel wanted at school.

As an educator, I can tell you that these measures are sometimes necessary to ensure safety, but overall, they have many, many negative effects on individual students. The research has overwhelmingly shown that multiple suspensions lead to expulsion, drop out, and prison. Educators often refer to the "suspension to prison" pipeline because research has shown us that this is the reality for many.

I've lost count, but Jason had been suspended at the very least 30 times by the 4th grade. I withdrew him from kindergarten a month early because the school told me that they were seriously considering expulsion. We were also told that he was no longer welcome at a separate after-school program that same year. These are pretty strong messages for a child. Personally, if I were repeatedly asked to leave school, I would never want to show my face there again.

ADHD presents itself in many different ways; however, children with ADHD struggle with self-regulation, impulsivity, and anger, and violence can be a "go-to" for them in the moment. When they are in a calmer space, people with ADHD are able to view situations more reasonably; however, their disability centers around an executive functioning disorder that makes thinking before acting difficult, and sometimes not even possible. Kids are working within these limitations, and instead of supporting and encouraging them, when they fail, we are removing them from the learning environment. I promise you the rejection and the negative messages internalized hurt more than the day off of school.

A POPULATION AT RISK

Our ADHD kids are a population at serious risk. I say "our" because kids with ADHD form a significant portion of our collective community. According to the American Psychiatric Association, approximately 8.4% of school-age children have ADHD (Parekh, 2017). Arguably not all of those with ADHD are ever diagnosed since behaviors such as inattentiveness and impulsivity can be attributed to other reasons. Those with ADHD form a large part of our society struggling with executive functioning tasks such as difficulty concentrating, engaging socially, following instructions, and more.

Children with ADHD are at a much higher risk for adverse outcomes, both in school and throughout their lives. They often begin by experiencing social isolation as their behavior is difficult to deal with, go on to feel rejection in the school setting through a series of negative events such as poor grades, suspension, and expulsion, and very often end up with a higher rate of divorce, substance abuse, incarceration, and suicide attempts (Harpin, 2019). Stated differently, the child that people whisper about and avoid inviting to birthday parties is at an increased risk for suicide after they experience multiple forms of rejection such as suspension, social isolation, and divorce.

A BRIEF HISTORY OF ADHD

As if it's not tough enough to deal with an executive function disorder, those with ADHD and their loved ones are often barraged with comments about how ADHD is a "new thing" or smug references about how there was no ADHD in their day; kids just played outside. The truth is that ADHD is about as modern as Ancient Greece.

Hippocrates, who lived from about 460 to 375 BC, documented cases, and theorized about a connection between the behaviors associated with ADHD, nutrition, and physical activity. Shakespeare mentions a person suffering from a "malady of attention" in his play "King Henry VIII, around 1613. In Dr. Weikard's work published between 1773 and 1775, he provides the most complete description of ADHD to date. A chapter of his book, *Der Phiosophische Arz*t, is called "Mangel der Aufmerksamkeit" or "Attention Deficit." While Weikard dispelled many medieval beliefs such as outside forces like astrology controlling behavior, he also perpetuated stereotypes that we are still struggling to move away from, such as ADHD being the result of a poor upbringing or general lack of discipline. In 1798 Sir Alexander Crichton of Scotland, physician to the Czar of Russia, referred to a condition that he called "disease of attention" whose sufferers had difficulty maintaining their focus on tasks or games. When John Locke wrote "Thoughts Concerning Education," he referred to students that cannot "keep their mind from straying." In 1832, Goethe described a boy, "Euphorion," who exhibited hyperactive behavior, showed little concern for consequences, and displayed excessive motor activity. The mention of ADHD continues consistently into the next century through the present time.

There were no theories discussed pointing to what we call "ADHD" in the 1800s; however, there are several mentions of the typically associated symptoms in case studies. Sir George Frederic provided a more comprehensive profile of some of the typical behaviors associated with ADHD in 1902. In a series of three lectures, he describes his study of 43 children that showed a lack of ability to maintain attention while exhibiting difficulty self-regulating, modifying their behavior based on consequences, and in many cases displaying violent behaviors. He further noted that this condition was not tied to intellectual ability, suggested that more boys than girls presented symptoms, and explored the possibility of the condition being hereditary.

Benzedrine was given to children for headaches by Dr. Charles Bradley in Rhode Island in the early 20th century. He noted that a side effect of the amphetamine administered was increased performance in school due to enhanced focus. Another amphetamine, Ritalin, became available in 1954 for the treatment of the symptoms associated with ADHD. Ritalin is said to have gotten its name from the wife of Leandro Panizzon, a Swedish doctor chemist, who tested it on his wife Marguerite, known as "Rita."

Even though we've been talking about ADHD since Ancient Greece, we've only called it "ADHD" since the 1980s. The American Psychiatric Association began the use of the names "ADD" and "ADHD." We still continue to develop our understanding of the types or presentations of ADHD and to expand our knowledge of medications that help to manage symptoms.

Now that we know that ADHD is not "new," why do we hear more and more about it? There is a combination of factors that are contributing to an increase in diagnoses. First of all, people are becoming more aware. The child that was "a defiant rebel" and the kids that had "ants in their pants" when I was growing up are now being referred to their pediatrician to discuss the possibility of ADHD. Simply put, not that many people knew what ADHD was or that their kid could have it. Increased media attention, access to information, and open dialogue about mental health and disabilities have all contributed to this increase in awareness. At this point, most everyone's heard of ADHD, but not that many people really understand it. There is still a lot of mystery around its causes, systems, treatment, etc.

Many would argue that our modern life contributes to an increased likelihood for children to have or develop ADHD. They point out that our food supply is riddled with chemicals and that we don't even know the extent of their damage. Others question the insane amount of screen time that most of our society is exposed to and arguably addicted to, including our youngest members. They point to lowering rates of our attention span across age levels as an indicator that our hyper exposure to sound bites is creating an increase in ADHD.

Unfortunately, it takes society hundreds of years to recognize, understand, create awareness, and provide hope to people that suffer from disabilities, particularly when they are invisible. At this point, we don't have all of the answers, but we are beginning to validate ADHD, and the sooner we begin to seek to understand, to listen, to ask questions, to collaborate—as parents, children, teachers, and health care providers— the better for our children.

THE CHALLENGES FACED BY ADHD LEARNERS IN SCHOOLS TODAY

Overwhelmingly, our population of children with ADHD is not faring well in the United States' education system. This situation inspired me to research international models and initiate global conversations among parents and educators about ADHD through the hashtag #ADHDGlobalConvo on Twitter, a Facebook group called #ADHD-GlobalConvo, and webinars. Unfortunately, what I found was a common thread in educators across several countries who recognized that their school system was not adequately supporting children with ADHD. I also connected with parents across the world who are struggling to deal with challenging behaviors at home and at school, teachers who do not feel supported or in many cases even equipped to support students, and above all, kids who are really, really struggling. Being in school, as we have designed it, is really hard for children with ADHD.

As with many children with ADHD, entering "regular school" was a very difficult period for Jason. He attended a traditional school that was somewhat authoritarian in its approach. I thought that a smaller school and structured environment would help Jason. Boy, was I wrong. Looking back, I can't even believe that I thought that was a good idea. That school was great for my daughters but a nightmare for Jason. Initially, he did well; he was very enthusiastic about going to school and proud to be a learner. I remember him balking at staying home sick because he was "missing out on learning." There was definitely a glorious honeymoon phase, but it ended abruptly and badly.

Ultimately Jason could not handle the lack of movement and choice that most school settings provide. He began to seek ways to get his energy out, such as pretending to be a bunny and hopping around the classroom during instruction. When he was bored, he would often throw things or purposely make a mess, such as emptying bookshelves. He became frustrated and frequently violent to other children.

Obviously, this behavior was not acceptable. The teacher would do everything that she could to calm him. She honestly did go above and beyond in terms of trying to establish a rapport with Jason and providing him with frequent positive feedback. Many interventions were voluntarily implemented by his teacher. Unfortunately, it was not enough support for Jason at that age, and the behavior incidents continued.

The school's policies were strict, and when Jason began to have frequent interaction with the administration, he became very defiant. The more they tried to impose consequences, the more Jason seemed to stop caring about pleasing them and the scenes intensified. He began to tell me that he didn't like school. That was heartbreaking and scary news to me. How could a little boy who was so excited about school and learning decide that he didn't like school so quickly? What would become of my son if he stopped caring about school?

School for many kids with ADHD can be a lot like trying to fit a square-shaped peg into a round hole. In general, school has not worked well for Jason thus far. Over the years, there have been many, many incidents of Jason hitting, running away, distracting others, hurting others, not being on task, not completing work, etc. Academically, I don't feel that Jason has been able to reach his potential in the school environments that he's been in. An example of this would be that even though he's highly gifted in math and thinks about mathematical theories in his spare time, he barely passes math most of the time.

"When I'm in class, sometimes I feel like it's just too much going on and it makes me feel like I want to keep moving or do something else. Even sometimes when I walk into my classroom I right away feel unfocused. Everyone's making noise and there's a bunch of kids and all of that commotion makes me feel annoyed. I really try to sit at my desk but I can't sit still because I'm not very good at being still, I always have to move, and then all of the noise and people and talking makes me frustrated. I get in trouble a lot and have to go to the counselor's office. I get mad that my teacher asks me to leave a lot but I like to be in the counselor's office better really. It's quiet in there

except for sometimes there are other little kids that act basically how I acted in first grade but sometimes I can help the counselor calm them down."

Having a child with ADHD in school for a parent can feel like carrying a boulder while swimming against the current. It takes a lot of meetings, accommodations, and the cooperation from a team of teachers, counselors, administration, and myself for him to even function at school and to minimize how often he "gets in trouble." Unfortunately, most parents do not have access to an alternative. Some families have chosen to homeschool or found homeschool cooperatives in their areas. Personally, where I live, some schools look amazing and are designed for children with ADHD, but their tuition is over $20,000 per year. Jason still begs me to homeschool him, which makes me sad because I'm a teacher, but I cannot afford to leave my job to teach him at home.

Many kids with ADHD are on a vicious cycle of getting in trouble because they can't self-regulate well enough to succeed in the classroom. This cycle is hard on everyone involved. Parents are frazzled by phone calls. You understand that the school has to call, but it's very overwhelming to get (constant) phone calls about behavior that, in all honesty, you can't control either. It's demoralizing and discouraging to parents. We don't know what to do. We're scared, we're worried, we're embarrassed, etc.—pretty much all at once. Teachers are overwhelmed with 20, 30, and yes, 40 kids in a classroom with multiple needs, personalities, learning differences, etc. Discipline policies generally do not differentiate when it comes to discipline consequences, meaning that a disproportionate number of kids with special needs end up suspended and even expelled. Obviously, systemically there are some major problems with this picture, but above all, the child is suffering because we, the adults, are not adequately supporting them.

POINTS TO PONDER

- If ADHD is a neurodevelopment disorder that affects executive functioning in the brain, why are kids regularly punished for exhibiting behaviors associated with this condition? Is this just?
- Do we adequately address a disability when it is visible?
- Are there laws in place to protect and to support kids with ADHD?

∼

IEPS & 504S ARE ONLY AS EFFECTIVE AS THEIR IMPLEMENTATION

Individual Education Plans (IEPs) and 504 Plans are documents that legally obligate schools to provide specific support to a particular child with a disability's needs. If the child does not receive the modifications and accommodations detailed in this document, parents and guardians have recourse through the legal system. On the surface, this may seem like problem solved—kids with disabilities get a document that lays out the specific support that they need, and it is legally binding.

In reality, this is not what is happening in all too many cases. It can be a long and confusing road to get an IEP or 504 for a child with ADHD. Jason still doesn't have one. ADHD is not covered as a disability under The Individuals with Disabilities Education Act (IDEA) from 1975, except as under the category of Other Health Impaired (OHI). Generally, in order to qualify, children have to have a separate learning disability that has caused them to be 1.5 years behind grade level. In Jason's case, he's not below grade level because he doesn't have a learning disability. He's gifted, which I dare say works to his disadvantage in terms of receiving legal protection for the support that he needs to be successful.

I asked for Jason to be evaluated for Special Education services through an IEP. He was evaluated, but the evaluator apparently observed Jason on a good day. He described an idyllic scene where Jason was reading in a group with his peers. His report stated that Jason's behavior did not warrant receiving services because he had demonstrated that he was able to control himself and to be productive in class. I have no idea how the fact that Jason had multiple, and very serious, incidents of disruption and hyperactivity in class was not taken into account. Maybe it was but dismissed as "bad" conduct. I really don't know how the conclusion was arrived at, but what I can tell you is that when a person in a professional role told me that an evaluation found that Jason did not qualify for special services, I was really at a loss.

Kids with ADHD most often receive modifications and accommodations under a 504 Plan from the Rehabilitation Act of 1973, meaning that they receive all of their instruction in a general education classroom and do not receive transitional services to adulthood. I've requested an evaluation for a 504 Plan for Jason twice, and both times, he was denied based on the school's evaluation. I could have pursued this by filing a grievance with the school district; however, based on the circumstances at the time, I did not choose to do this. Whether a real or perceived fear, like many other parents, I was afraid to "push" too hard for fear of creating an adversarial relationship with the school.

Despite their technical differences from a legal standpoint, both documents play an almost identical role in the daily lives of children with ADHD at school. They both provide a combination of "accommodations" that detail changes to accessing instruction and "modifications" that provide for changes in the content of what is learned. An "accommodation" could be to allow a student to sit in an area with minimal distractions or to take sensory breaks. Examples of "modifications" would be to allow a child to create an outline rather than an essay or changing a required reading for a less complex one.

Children who have the benefit of having these documents in place have a clearly written framework to support them. Even if allowing a student additional time to complete assignments is against a teacher's classroom policy, or if they disagree with a student using the textbook during a test, IEP's and 504's must be followed with fidelity. In an ideal world, IEP's and 504's are followed, and it is actually the law that they must be; however, there are many cases currently in litigation over this matter. Additionally, many, many families do not have the information or resources to fight this in court. We will unfortunately never have accurate data on the number of parents who feel that their child's IEP or 504 is not being followed with fidelity.

In my view, in order for these documents to have real meaning, teachers have to have an understanding of what limitations ADHD comes with and empathy for learners working within these limitations. Overall I would prefer for a teacher to establish a positive working relationship with my son than to follow a list of supports that they may not even agree with. An IEP or a 504 is a potentially powerful tool in supporting kids, but it does not stand alone. Meaningful support lies in the willingness of a teacher to observe a child with an open heart and to have the knowledge needed to be a responsive educator. This level of collaboration between teachers and students is what will really make the difference for our children with ADHD.

IEP vs 504	Individualized Education Plan (IEP)	Section 504 Plan
Type of law	Special Education - Individuals with Disabilities Act (IDEA)	Civil Rights - Rehabilitation Act of 1973
Department	Department of Education	Office of Civil Rights
Requirements for eligibility	Has a disability that: a) meets criteria under IDEA, b) significantly impacts educational performance, and c) requires specialized services	Has a disability that significantly impacts a major life function
What is typically included?	Specialized education services, accommodations, related services	Accommodations, modifications, and related services
Age limits	IEP offered through 12th grade or until age 21 when required	No age limits with a 504 plan
Where is the plan used?	Educationally, through the 12th grade. Does not transfer to college	School, work, and college. Eligibility and plan creation occurrs at each institution
Discipline	A Manifestation Determination meeting must be held to determine if the offense is a manifestation of the disability by the 10th day of suspension. Services are required during long-term suspension	A Manifestation Determination meeting must be held to determine if the offense is a manifestation of the disability by the 10th day of suspension. May require reevaluation

www.schoolpsychologistfiles.com

©School Psychologist Files 2020 Printed with permission.

IMPACT ON SOCIETY

> "ADHD is real and valid. The sooner we recognize the patterns and learn to work with these kids, the better assured we will be that they as adults will be healthy members of society."
>
> — *RHONDA VAN DIEST*

If we are not moved to understand our population with ADHD out of compassion, consider the costs associated in terms of healthcare, school resources, the prison system, and more. ADHD affects many areas of social and public policy. In education, we see a large population that is at increased risk of dropping out, suspension, expulsion, and generally requires special education services. Our adoption and foster care systems are faced with placing a disproportionate number of children with ADHD, largely due to behavior issues compounded by trauma and a lack of services received. People with ADHD commit more crimes, burdening our prison system. Substance abuse is more prevalent among those diagnosed with ADHD. It is impossible to accurately state the amount, in dollars, that the increase in associated services costs taxpayers (Hinshaw, Peele, & Danielson, 1999). At some point, we must come to terms with the fact that those with ADHD suffer from an executive function disorder and that ADHD affects all of us.

REFLECTION POINTS

Let's continue this conversation and learn from one another. Share your thoughts in a tweet with the hashtag #ADHDGlobalConvo and feel free to mention me directly @BiscottiNicole.

- What does it feel like to be a child in a classroom with ADHD in a society that barely recognizes it?
- What are the possible barriers to a child with ADHD having an IEP or 504 Plan in place?
- What gaps of support do you see around you in education for children with ADHD? For teachers? For parents?

ADHD IN THE CLASSROOM: THE MANY FACES OF ADHD

POINTS TO PONDER

- How do I know if a student has ADHD?
- What are the different types of ADHD?
- What is the teacher's role in diagnosis and what are their responsibilities to that student?

∽

"I remember I was at my preschool and I was mad, I think because I just wanted to play with Legos but some other kid kept saying "no." I grabbed a big ruler and just started hitting everything I could see. I was about to explode and I was running and the teachers were chasing me. It's not like I wanted to do that or it's not like this was my way to get my anger out. I was just so angry I didn't even know what I was doing and at that point I was just still mad at the kid."

When Jason was in preschool, I would receive anywhere from 1-6 incident reports most days about Jason's behavior. They always described him as either running away or attacking something or someone. These incidents were also always preceded by him becoming angry very quickly, usually over a perceived injustice or someone in his space, and they always had pretty horrible scenes. It was a pretty constant situation, despite meetings, interventions, conversations, and me trying everything that I could think of at home. I had a serious parenting dilemma of being stricter as opposed to being more understanding. I went back and forth and was basically ineffective in correcting any of his poor behavior.

> **Child's Full Name:** Jason Vargas **Classroom:** Room B
>
> ☒ Behavioral – *verbal*
> ☒ Behavioral – *physical*
> ☐ Accident – with injury
> ☐ Accident – without injury
> ☐ Parent Conflict
> ☐ Other
>
> **Date of Incident:** 5/11/15 **Location:** Room U **Time of Incident:** 7:50
>
> **Description of Incident:** I sat down at the table to eat breakfast with the children. Jason was sitting next to me and was already yelling, chanting and spitting. I told Jason "You are spitting in my food. If you are done eating, you can
>
> **Action Taken:** Reported to management
>
> **Documented By:** ▮▮▮▮▮ **Witnesses:** ▮▮▮▮▮
>
> **Notifications:**
> ☒ Parent/ Guardian
> ☒ SF Management
> ☐ Dir. of Children's Service
> ☐ Sr. Director of Facilities
> ☐ Case Manager
> ☐ CPS
>
> **KC Manager:** ▮▮▮▮▮ **Date:** 5/11/15
>
> **Parent Signature:** _____ **Date:** _____

At a certain point, I became basically numb and stopped taking any action at all. I honestly didn't know what to do. My pediatrician said that it was too early to diagnose him. The preschool that Jason attended was a teaching facility with highly trained personnel in early childhood development. They advised that it was too early to tell if his behavior was related to his age or if it would continue as he went to school. I knew something was wrong, and I feared for my son, but I felt powerless and without any way to help him.

We had meetings at the preschool to discuss Jason's behavior and possible interventions. They really put a lot of effort into working with Jason. The meetings were difficult for me because, on the one hand, I wanted to be informed, but on the other, they sometimes felt more like a 45-minute source of shame, stress, and embarrassment that ultimately left me feeling more disempowered.

This is the real me—Jason's mom in all of my transparency. I was not dealing with someone else's child professionally, but one of my own personally. This was my baby. I was grateful to the school for meeting with me and for all of the obvious effort going into my child; however, I was embarrassed by his behavior and felt scared and powerless to affect any change in the situation. I have seen this dynamic over the years when I call parents to discuss different behavior or achievement challenges. They almost always want to apologize. As a mom who has been there, and sometimes still is there, I know that feeling all too well. As educators, we can form impactful partnerships with parents by assuring them that we are all part of a team of support for their child.

DIAGNOSIS

POINTS TO PONDER

- What is ADHD?
- Why do so many kids seem to have it?
- What are the risks associated? How are kids with ADHD served in schools?
- How does this affect everyone in society?

The American Psychiatric Association lists ADHD as a diagnosis in *The American Psychiatric Association's Diagnostic and Statistical Manual of Mental Disorders*, a guide that is used internationally. ADHD is defined as "a persistent pattern of inattention and/or hyperactivity-impulsivity that interferes with functioning or development." There are no biomarkers for ADHD; diagnoses are made based on referrals resulting from parents' and teachers' observations (Kim, King, & Jennings, 2019). Both clinical and psychosocial factors are taken into account when evaluating for ADHD. Typically multiple assessments are used before arriving at a diagnosis, which generally entails clinical interviews and questionnaires filled out by parents and educators.

Having a diagnosis early on would have greatly lessened Jason's suffering. I would have known what we were up against, and the process of understanding would have begun much sooner. I would have understood that Jason's "problems" had a label, and I could have understood that he was part of 8.4% of kids that are constantly in trouble at school for being off task, speaking out of turn, not staying in their seat, hitting, and the list goes on (Parekh, 2017). At the very minimum, I would have felt validated in sensing that Jason's behaviors were really more than he could always control. If Jason had a diagnosis, I would have had an answer for people when they commented about how "bad" Jason was that could have saved his dignity and increased understanding.

In essence, I was searching for a label. There is a lot of discussion about labels and how people avoid them or are afraid of their child having one. Personally, I wanted a label desperately. I felt that once Jason's behavior had a name, I could follow a prescribed approach to solving the problem. In reality, that was only partially true. Jason's ultimate diagnosis of ADHD with ODD gave me a name to search on Google and to read about, but the journey was only beginning.

I was diagnosed with ADHD twice. I didn't believe the first doctor who told me, and I had a whole theory that ADHD was just something they invented to make you pay for medicine, but then the second doctor told me I had it."

— SOLANGE KNOWLES

I can tell you with great certainty that my little ADHDer had very different behaviors from a young age. The intensity, frequency, and disconnect that Jason's acting out had from preschool was very different than most other children. Considering that ADHDers usually stand out with some pretty noticeable behaviors and receive a lot of negative attention, how can we not help them to understand themselves better? I wish I could have shielded Jason from the almost daily incidents where he was in trouble, but that wasn't possible. I also wish that I could have protected him from noticing that he acted differently than most other children, but that was equally impossible since it was usually him running out the door, fighting, or throwing things. Those are the visible symptoms of his condition; I can't even begin to know how he felt internally at preschool.

Getting a label for Jason's condition was a gift to me as a parent because it gave me something that I could learn about and a framework to understand and approach his behavior. Jason shares, *"When I was little and I heard that I had ADHD I didn't really know what that meant exactly but I guessed that something was making it hard for me to behave not just like I didn't want to behave because I really actually did."*

The medical community does not generally diagnose ADHD before a child is approximately seven years old. One of the main reasons for this is that the behaviors presented with ADHD are similar to many of the typical behaviors of small children. A lot of children have trouble maintaining focus, managing a large amount of energy, and with impulse control. Fortunately, many of these children will grow up and Jason's preschool teacher, Jennifer Hicks, recalls that "other than the outbursts, Jason's behavior was within the normal range for a preschooler boy." Miss Jennifer further said that "Jason's behavior issues were not regularly different than that of other children his age. His outbursts were frequent but not continuous throughout the day. Jason's ability to express himself was always above grade level in terms of vocabulary, focus on conversation, and self-awareness. It is hard to separate behaviors that are in response to situations versus inherent in the child at the preschool level. In preschool, ADHD is not something teachers are looking for." Although as a parent, I was noticing behaviors that seemed extreme to me, the teachers did not seem alarmed or to feel that this was necessarily an indication of ADHD.

Another reason for waiting to be diagnosed until a child is school age is directly related to the need for observation in the school setting. Because ADHD refers to a pattern of behavior across different settings, there must be a presentation of inattentiveness, hyperactivity, and impulse control both at school and at home. Teachers play a critical role in identifying children with ADHD by knowing the signs and communicating possible concerns with families and school counselors. A child quite literally needs a team of their parents, teachers, and health care professionals to be identified, which is the first step to receiving critical support.

In terms of detection, we often run into popular misconceptions about ADHD. To help kids, educators need to familiarize themselves with the signs so that complete evaluations can be done as early as possible. Most people expect for a child with ADHD to have trouble focusing on a task. When Jason was young, I thought that the fact that my son was able to focus, even hyper-focus on tasks like building intricate structures, must mean that he did not have ADHD. I also had no idea that impulsivity was such a huge red flag—and Jason had plenty of impulsivity.

People with ADHD often have extreme focus, in fact. When Jason was smaller, this was apparent with his intent way of building for hours. As he's gotten older, I've seen the same thing happen with Legos and his iPad. He is capable of going into what looks from the outside like a zone where he is completely involved with a task that holds his interest for an almost indefinite amount of time. Miss. Jennifer also shares, "Although behavior issues were apparent, Jason was able to engage and attend to things in an extremely focused manner." Jason regularly spent 30-45 minutes at a time on diverse activities such as painting or other forms of creative play. At times he was even hyper-focused on a task, particularly when building. He would often spend hours on his buildings. They were very intricate and symmetrical structures such as airports complete with several feet of runways.

Kathleen Nadeau, Ph.D. puts it very succinctly in her book, *ADD-Friendly Ways to Organize Your Life*, "People who think ADHD means having a short attention span misunderstand what ADHD is. A better way to look at it is that people with ADHD have a dysregulated attention system." Another way to state this is that ADHD is a "disorder of attention" rather than an actual "deficit of attention." This insight provided me with a lot of clarity. Jason seems to go back and forth from a hyper-focused, almost trance-like state, to can't stop moving and struggles to maintain eye contact during a conversation.

∽

KEY INSIGHTS...

1. Not ALL kids that are hyper, disorganized, disruptive, or inattentive have ADHD.
2. ADHD symptoms vary greatly; each child has a unique combination of symptoms which is often accompanied by a comorbidity such as a learning challenge.
3. ADHD is *invisible* to us, but still very real. We just cannot view the brain.
4. ADHD is diagnosed by medical professionals based on a team effort between teachers, parents, and doctors.
5. A key to diagnosing ADHD is examining *patterns* of behavior in *different* settings.

～

THE WAYS THAT ADHD CAN LOOK

Picture a room with 1,000 TVs with each TV showing something different.

Now try and concentrate on just one TV without getting distracted."

— DAMIAN DAVIKING AIRD

Two points are important to keep in mind as we discuss the characteristics of ADHD. One is that every child will display different behaviors in a wholly unique combination. Some children tend to struggle with inattentive behaviors, while others are more inclined toward hyperactive/impulsive behavior. The second is that ADHD is diagnosed by a pattern of behavior. This is important to remember because almost all children exhibit these behaviors in different settings and to differing levels of intensity. Children with ADHD will consistently show these behaviors no matter where they are: home, school, and other social settings.

Inattention

"Sometimes I don't do very well when the teacher is talking because they say too many things at one time and it just confuses me. Like I'm really good at math but when they tell me a lot of steps and all of that I get lost so I just start thinking about other stuff. I usually just think of random stuff like one thing and then a minute later something totally different. I actually think about a lot of stuff at once normally. Most of it doesn't really make sense so I just forget about it later."

Inattentiveness can be one of the more difficult signs of ADHD to notice in a classroom setting. Unfortunately, the child that is disruptive with hyperactive and impulsive behavior generally takes center stage. Their inattentive counterparts, and their needs, can easily fly under a teacher's radar. We have to be intentional about observing students to have a better chance of identifying inattentiveness. Sometimes students are quiet and compliant in class and just seem to make careless mistakes or not able to follow instructions without additional prompts. We can easily think that students like this are having difficulty *understanding* rather than *focusing*.

 I am not absentminded. It is the presence of mind that makes me unaware of everything else."

— *G.K. CHESTERTON*

Another way that inattentiveness can manifest is through children having difficulty with organization and following through with details. Sadly, children can be chastised, scolded, and even punished for being "careless" or "not caring" about their schoolwork. Children with inattentiveness can also be called "lazy" because they may resist doing complex tasks or tasks that require focus. Frequently losing things such as backpacks, books, and school supplies can also be a symptom of ADHD. It's important to notice if these behaviors are happening in multiple settings and if there is an established pattern over time.

Inattentiveness accounts for one of the areas in which children with ADHD run into problems with compliance in the classroom setting. At times they display avoidance behaviors such as not taking notes when the rest of the class is, not being on task, not following through with directions, tardiness, taking a long time to "use the restroom," not coming to class, etc. It's easy to become frustrated when you teach upwards of thirty children because the tendency is to want everyone to follow directions to facilitate instruction.

Children that are not following through may seem to be quietly defiant or refusing to comply, but in many cases, when we look at the "why," we realize that they are feeling confused, overwhelmed, or having difficulty focusing. Unfortunately, because these behaviors are not acceptable in the classroom setting, as children progress through school, they are all too often facing years of negative feedback and punitive measures. Repeated negative messages and the awareness of being not able to meet behavioral and academic standards can have detrimental effects on the self-esteem and self-efficacy of ADHD learners.

Impulsivity

"My mom said that impulsivity is not thinking about things before I do them. I told her she kind of just explained ME. It gets me in trouble in school because if I'm mad or another student makes me mad I probably want to hit that student or throw something or just express my anger. I know I'm not supposed to but I only realize that after I've already done it. When I'm mad nothing else matters, I just want to express my anger."

"Another example of how this causes me problems is that I know I like to work in groups with my friends but being honest here I don't do very good work in groups. It's fun because I get to be with friends and laugh a lot but then sometimes they don't like me because I don't act very well in school. I get hyper and distracted and the problem with me is that I don't stop myself before I start being hyper and when I'm done being like that I know I shouldn't have acted that way or been in a group because I get like that. Maybe I should just be in groups for playing outside and sports and stuff because I actually love being in groups for sports and stuff."

I would say that Jason's impulsivity gets him into the most trouble socially and in school. Impulsivity in children with ADHD often looks like not being able to wait for a turn, blurting out at inappropriate times in class, and not respecting others' space. The ability to control our impulses speaks to the space between feeling and acting. This space, in real terms, is the time needed to avoid an unpleasant external outcome between yourself and others based on an internal emotional overreaction.

Jason wants very much to be liked and to be accepted. When he's calm, he's empathetic and is careful about not hurting others' feelings and showing respect to those around him. He cognitively understands social cues and norms, but he struggles in the moment, particularly if he's experiencing strong emotions at the time. For example, Jason knows he should wait to speak in class, but if the teacher is not giving him a turn, he will often talk anyway, particularly if he is excited or worried about something. Another common scenario is that he becomes frustrated and wants to be heard and forgets all about respecting people's personal space, which can be very uncomfortable to other children. Children that behave this way are often called "rude" or "immature" when, in fact, they are working within the constraints of a neurological disorder.

Hyperactivity

"When I thought about this I realized I'm pretty much the most hyper person ever probably. I move around like more than half of the time in my life. I pretty much never stop moving. In class I get up, I lift my chair a little, I move around, it just really never stops. I don't, like, walk around the room but I wish I could, to be honest. When I was little I did but we're not going to talk about that right now because I was little and sometimes little kids do stuff like that. Basically I just need a space that I can move in and then it's ok. Sometimes it's distracting to other kids but over time they kind of just get used to it. I don't even really notice that I'm moving or fidgeting. Sometimes it helps me concentrate but sometimes I just do it because I always do."

Hyperactivity is a tough symptom to recognize even though it's an obvious easy behavior to identify. We don't need to describe hyperactivity; if you're a teacher or parent, you've undoubtedly seen children being hyper. Little kids that can't seem to sit still, get out of their seats, pick on the person next to them because they're bored, run in instead of walk, talk a lot, etc., are not hard to find. In fact, almost all little kids behave this way sometimes. Kids with ADHD take these behaviors a few steps farther, however.

Hyperactivity in Jason looks like he literally cannot sit still. When you talk to Jason, he is usually moving around in his seat, doing interesting yoga-like poses, blinking, or playing with an object. He sometimes seems to be driven by a motor that doesn't stop. On top of the almost constant movement, there are times when he needs to go for a short run or bike ride to release energy. As he's grown, he's learned to recognize the additional energy bursts as a need for movement, and he'll self-advocate by telling me that he needs to have a movement break. There is no real "middle ground" with Jason's energy level. Unless he's tired, he's usually either moving or hyper-focused on a task.

Jason also makes noise almost constantly, which I tend to feel like is for "no reason." In reality, of course, like all behavior, his making noises serves a purpose or "function." He has so much energy that making noises is a release for him. When he does not have the flexibility to move, he becomes frustrated and is very likely to act out. When he was little, this would look like him "suddenly" throwing pencils when the class was sitting at their desks listening. Again, it's important to remember that ADHD is consistent patterns of behaviors in different settings. Understanding this insight can help educators to know when a child is being hyperactive within what is typical for them as opposed to possibly showing signs of ADHD.

ADHD symptoms can be manifested by behaviors such as:	
Inattention	an inability to comply with basic classroom expectations
	not "following along" or taking notes in class
	being distracted
	daydreaming
	disorganization
	having a resistance to tasks that require focus
	avoiding
Impulsivity	difficulty with social cues
	intruding upon others' physical and emotional space
	blurting out answers or comments in class
	acting without any thought about consequences
	having outbursts
	frequent emotional displays
Hyperactivity	constantly moving and fidgeting
	preferring kinesthetic learning methods
	expressing a "need" to move almost all of the time
	becoming frustrated or acting out when made to sit still
	talking and making noises excessively

ADHD and Psychiatric Comorbidities

ADHD symptoms can be further confused because many children with ADHD also have a comorbidity such as a learning disability, anxiety, oppositional defiance disorder, sensory hypersensitivity, etc. Comorbidities can add to the confusion and misconceptions; an estimated one-third of the children with ADHD have a learning disability, which causes many people to assume that all children with ADHD have learning disabilities. Similarly, out of the most prevalent comorbidities, Oppositional Defiance Disorder (ODD) is the most common, but again, not all children with ADHD have ODD.

The confusion of comorbidities is enhanced by the often overlapping symptoms. For example, Jason becomes frustrated very quickly when he can't move and begins to act out because he has ADHD. Since Jason also has ODD, if an adult approaches him in an authoritarian way, he is likely to become defiant, which could look like him running away across campus. Many children struggle to maintain focus because of their ADHD, while they also face additional challenges due to a learning disability. Children with ADHD have more stimulation in the cortices of the brain in a resting state, and a comorbidity of Sensory Hypersensitivity has been correlated with increased aggression and adverse outcomes in social settings as well as school (Ghanizadeh, 2011). Jason describes this by sharing that sometimes when he goes into his classroom, he feels immediately angry because the lights are too bright and the kids are too noisy.

The Strengths of ADHD

"ADHD makes me creative. I love building games and building stuff. I've been like that ever since I was little. I started with big blocks and now I'm pretty much just into video games where you can create ships and fortresses and stuff. I'm also really good at math. I have very creative ways to get answers. I also think of creative strategies to do stuff. My brain goes really fast, it just can't function in school. I really understand other kids that have ADHD or other problems. I know they're good people and I care about them a lot and want to help them."

If you consider the stereotypical "creative type" and "absent-minded genius," they are characterized by being disorganized, hyper-focused, having inconsistent personal lives, social difficulties, intensity, and impulsivity. People with ADHD have a high sense of creativity and are definitely not limited to "the box." They tend to be unconventional in their thinking patterns, perceptions, and their experience of the world is from a different perspective allowing them to see possibilities that others miss. Their ability to hyperfocus is a trait that they can leverage to their advantage and pushes their talents to a heightened level. Their energy can also be an asset, particularly in sports such as Michael Phelps, U.S. Olympic Swimmer and ADHDer.

It has often been claimed that many of the world's geniuses had ADHD, such as Thomas Edison and Albert Einstein, both brilliant, innovative, and energetic. We can't have a reliable diagnosis of historical figures; however, psychologists and historians draw reasonable conclusions based on accounts of the person's life. For example, it is well documented that Leonardo da Vinci was restless, had erratic sleeping patterns, an inconsistent personal life, and was held back professionally by a lack of organization and reliability with clients. Others that worked with him, such as Marcantonio Della Torre, shared similar concerns about his inability to finish projects but recognized that it was partly due to his hyperfocus on his art. Marcantonio Della Torre said that DaVinci possessed an attention to detail that was so singular it impeded his ability to finish projects. Da Vinci shared about his difficulty with time management and focus in his journal when he wrote, "It is easier to resist at the beginning than at the end." His creative masterpiece, "The Mona Lisa," took him four years to paint. Although Leonardo da Vinci has been immortalized by his legacy of creative genius, in his lifetime, his inconsistencies cost him the respect of his clients.

Pope Leone X employed Leonardo in 1514 but frustration took hold of the Pope's heart when he noticed Leonardo's inability to attend to his duties. In desperation, Leone X exclaimed: 'Alas! this man will never do anything, for he begins by thinking of the end of the work, before the beginning' (Vasari, 1996) Leonardo's presence in the Vatican lasted less than 3 years" (Catani, M., & Mazzarello, 2019).

A more modern example would be Dav Pilkey, who has ADHD and is the author of several popular children's books, including the *Captain Underpants* series. Dav began writing this series in the second grade while sitting in the hall for his disruptive behavior in class. His writing is wildly popular with children, and with his creative genius, he has been a trailblazer in the genre of graphic novels for kids. I smile when I see Jason enjoying his books. Ironically, they hold his attention far longer than other books.

MEDICATION

I personally feel like medication is a little bit like the elephant in the classroom. Teachers wonder if kids are on medication, should be on medication, are doing alright with medication, would please get medication, etc. We're, of course, generally not allowed to discuss medication since we are not medical professionals. Teachers, like the rest of society, also have differing views on children taking medication for ADHD. It's important for teachers to be familiar with ADHD medications and their side effects, however. I also would like to share about our experience with medication. Every family's story is different, but for many families, the decision to use medication is a tough one and includes long-term concerns.

As a parent, deciding to give Jason medication was a very difficult decision for me to arrive at. We have been fortunate that he has not needed it indefinitely. I was very afraid that the medicine would control Jason, and he wouldn't be the same child. I resisted medicine right up until the end. I tried everything that I could think of or google about. As a teacher-mom, I went to his school meetings armed with strategies to suggest...I may have even brought a few highlighted and bookmarked studies along. Every child is different, but in our case, there came a point when I realized that my son was suffering despite everyone's best effort and that his self-esteem was taking a huge hit. I cried about it for days but knew that it was time to try medication.

Jason was prescribed Concerta, a common drug for treating the symptoms of ADHD. My out-of-pocket cost was $289 under the insurance plan that I had at the time. Ironically, kids with ADHD are usually treated with stimulants, which have a calming effect on them. The list of possible side effects is pretty scary as it is with most stimulants. Stimulants can cause a host of problems such as sweating, heart problems, irritability, hallucinations, problems sleeping, and slowed growth. Jason experienced something pretty common: the rage hour.

Concerta has extended-release, so its effects would last Jason all day. He didn't need to go to the nurse's office in the middle of the day for another dose like children on other medications or doses that are effective for a shorter period. Jason did great in school on Concerta! He could focus, he completed assignments, he was learning and not getting into trouble. Instead of getting in trouble every day during writing time, he researched and wrote a beautiful report about the Pilgrims. For a child who rarely completed his work, this was a huge accomplishment.

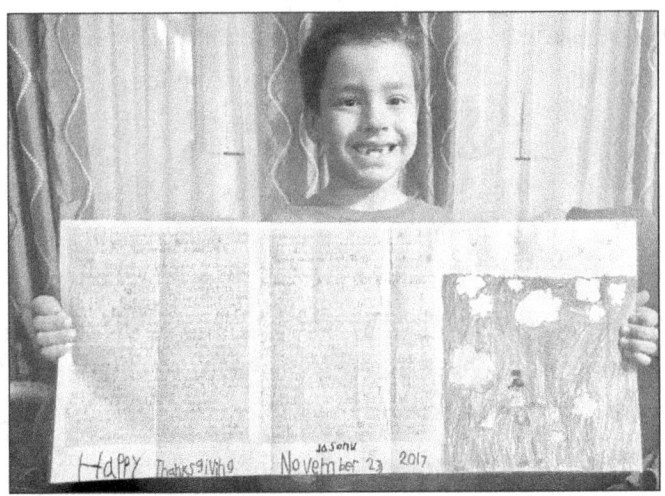

A proud Jason with his well-researched Pilgrim Project

Unfortunately, he also hardly ate and had an upset stomach a lot of the time while taking Concerta. I tried adjusting his diet several different ways but the stomach issues were always a challenge. Every evening he also had a hard time between 6-7 pm. Around that time, he would become very upset, unreasonable, and aggressive.

Jason himself was not a fan of taking medicine. He felt really good about his performance at school, but he didn't like the upset tummy so much, and he had reservations about the pill "taking him over." We had a lot of talks about it and watched videos to learn more together. We also used to talk about how ADHD would make it hard for him to pay attention or to not move so much because his brain worked really fast. When he took medication, it would help "ADHD" take a nap so that he could focus better at school. We learned together about the "come down" that he experienced nightly and planned for it by hanging out together and some days even managed to chuckle together at the way he behaved during it later on.

I am grateful that Jason did not have to stay on Concerta, but I am not overly confident because I know that he may have to take medication again. The treatment for ADHD is a combination approach of classroom interventions, parenting strategies, counseling, and sometimes medication. This is a delicate mix, and as Jason grows and develops, it has to be constantly modified. Input and feedback from Jason's teachers are invaluable in this process.

ADHD & THE CLASSROOM SETTING

"I prefer to distinguish ADD as attention abundance disorder.

Everything is just so interesting, remarkably at the same time."

— *FRANK COPPOLA, PRESIDENT, EXECUTIVE DIRECTOR, EDUTAINMENT, INC.*

As an educator and a mother, it pains me to acknowledge that the traditional classroom and ADHD are not a good match. Hours of sitting still, less and less recess all of the time, one size fits all instruction and assessments, and a culture of compliance are probably the worst-case scenarios for educating ADHDers. Large class sizes add to the challenges with their high level of stimulation and by making it easier to have ADHD symptoms go undetected. It is both very hard for kids with ADHD to be successful in school and very hard for teachers to effectively teach them in a traditional setting.

The assumption is typically made that the child is at fault for this mismatch, not the environment. This is why millions of kids with ADHD suffer from self-esteem issues and doubt their ability to achieve. School has been around for a long time; the apparent conclusion is that something is "wrong" with the child. Unfortunately, this has been a long-standing problem. Thomas Edison had this problem; his mother ultimately withdrew him from school due to his inability to adjust to the classroom environment. Thankfully, he continued to pursue knowledge.

One of the most heartbreaking aspects of Jason having ADHD is hearing him repeatedly express how he feels like he's not "good at school." He's even shared that he worries about his future in terms of being able to attend college. I've seen this as a teacher as well, over and over again. I teach high school, and unfortunately, many kids with ADHD have partially or even totally given up on school by that point. One of the most impactful ways that we can encourage growth in our students is by identifying and building upon their strengths. This is arguably even more critical with our kids with ADHD, considering that they are not typically well suited for success in the classroom setting and that they receive an inordinate amount of negative feedback.

PROFILES OF ADHD

An awareness of the ways that ADHD can present in the classroom setting allows us to assist with identification through referrals and to best support our students. Remember that ADHD can present a myriad of symptoms, which can be further complicated by the prevalence of comorbidities with ADHD. Here are a few examples of how ADHD can "look" in the classroom.

Malachai is the class clown. He's very popular and will do anything on a dare. He's also very good at sports. He used to work hard at practice and seemed to have boundless energy. He's in high school and finds it hard to maintain the minimum grades to be eligible to play on the basketball team. He has many friends, so sometimes he can get someone to do his work for him or give him the answers. He was benched for the season because he got caught cheating and can't play sports anymore. He's really depressed and feels humiliated. His parents think he's overreacting about losing the ability to play sports and should get more serious about school.

Katelyn is a pleasant child who never gets in trouble at school. She draws beautiful, detailed pictures in her notebooks but rarely takes notes in class. She's quiet, doesn't ask questions or call attention to herself, and seems a little shy with other kids. She passes her classes but doesn't have very high grades, mostly because she tends not to turn in big projects. When the teacher asks her if she needs more time to turn her project in, she shyly says "yes" but doesn't follow through.

Chris tries to hide that he cries a lot at school. He always seems to be in trouble, and the other kids joke about it a lot. He doesn't want them to think he's a baby. He would rather run away from the teacher than for anyone to see how upset he gets. He really wants the other kids to play with him, but he has trouble making friends. He's often frustrated because other children exclude him from games during recess. When he gets mad, he gets into fights a lot.

Armando struggles to pay attention in class. It all just seems too boring to him. He would really rather not have to go to school at all. He likes to work on cars and spends a lot of time on his phone researching different models. Cars hold his interest because they always have new models and broken cars are a challenge to be figured out. When he's working on cars, the day just flies by. His parents are pretty much always mad because his grades are terrible. He just feels like he can't learn sitting still listening to a teacher, and even when he tries really hard, he thinks about other stuff. He's fourteen, and at this point, there are a lot of things that he doesn't understand in his classes because he's always been this way. He feels ashamed that he doesn't make his parents proud.

I have had Malachai, Katelyn, Chris, and Armando in my class over and over again, and I imagine so have most educators. They have different names, of course, and their stories vary slightly, but the underlying struggle is consistent. The other consistent piece is that their struggles are all too often mistaken for discipline problems or go unnoticed.

REFLECTION POINTS

Let's continue this conversation and learn from one another. Share your thoughts in a tweet with the hashtag #ADHDGlobalConvo and feel free to mention me directly @BiscottiNicole.

- What are some of the behaviors in children that could stand out as possible ADHD?
- Who in my school do I speak with when a child seems like they might have ADHD?

"MAYBE HE'S POSSESSED?" ADDRESSING THE ADHD GAP IN TEACHER EDUCATION

POINTS TO PONDER

- What do I need to learn to be more effective with my students that have ADHD?
- How can I feel confident working with students with ADHD?
- What resources do I have for knowledge and support?
- What steps can I take to feel more confident and supported as a teacher of children with ADHD?

∼

THE LACK OF INFORMATION ABOUT ADHD

"What makes me sad is that the teachers never understand me and that other kids don't understand either. Sometimes I feel sad and angry at exactly the same time and the teachers just get *frustrated with me and put me in punishment or something. Then I just get more sad and more angry and then I feel like I'm about to explode and when I feel like that I don't think about what I'm doing anymore. I don't, like, think about if I'm going to hurt somebody or hurt something but I'm just so angry it doesn't really matter to me what I do at that time. I'm just angry and I just feel like I need to do something, like, to get the energy out of me and then afterwards I feel sad and bad about what I did and I feel like the teacher is mad at me. I realize at the end it felt like I was turned off but somebody or something was still moving me and then I realized what I did and I started feeling so sad and angry and I wish I could be good. Like I know it's possible to be good but at the same time it's impossible for me but I still know it's possible for me, I just can't seem to do it. Sometimes I feel ashamed of what I did and of my actions and I wish I could just, like, reverse it."*

There are times when Jason seems driven completely by emotions that those around him struggle to understand. When he is in this mode, it is very difficult to reason with him. I have found that those closest to him are the only successful ones. The teachers and administrators who have invested their time and energy to form a relationship have had the advantage that Jason will noticeably calm down in their presence. From the outside, it seems that Jason finds comfort in my presence and the presence of other adults that he feels very close to in these moments. The only other thing that works is allowing him a quiet place to settle down. This is often key for him because any further stimulation just feeds into his overabundance of energy. I always think of it as giving him a safe place to land.

"For some reason I started feeling mad and bored one day because we were learning about something stupid that I really didn't care about. I felt so much energy in me and I just wanted to get it out. I started running around the room then I got the microphone thing to

talk on the speaker in the classroom and I started just yelling at the top of my lungs. That wasn't my go to to get it out that way but I was already mad so that's what I did. I saw that the class was plugging their ears and I knew that since they were plugging their ears they weren't going to really like me or be my friend but I just felt like I didn't care right then and kept going. Then the teacher turned it off from her laptop so I grabbed a kid's water bottle and started running fast around the classroom and then I finally got caught and I had to sit in another classroom."

During one conversation, Jason's teacher expressed her frustration and how she had sincerely tried so many things, and nothing was working. I switched into a listener in the conversation and tried to lend her support. I am a teacher and can only begin to imagine how hard it would be to have Jason in my class. I have a lot of empathy and appreciation for his teachers because I know what it's like to be in their shoes. She began telling me about how she was so worried about Jason that she prayed for him. We were sitting in a public school, so that comment seemed a little out of place, but I felt her sincerity and took it in stride. What did alarm me was when she went on to say that she was concerned that he might be possessed by the devil. I am not kidding.

I have found myself in the uncomfortable position of explaining ADHD to teachers many times. This is awkward for me because I am by no means an expert on the subject. The other problem with this is that I don't want to seem like I'm telling the teacher how they should conduct their classroom or asking for special treatment for my child. The problem is that many teachers do not have sufficient training in this area, myself included. I only learned more about the condition because of Jason. We have adopted the Inclusion Model without adequate training for general education teachers. A study by Lawrence, Estrada, and McCormick published in *The Journal of*

Pediatric Nursing in 2017 showed that most teachers receive training in ADHD from professional development and through peer learning rather than from their formal education. The study further concluded that teachers would benefit from additional formal training on meeting the needs of students with ADHD. Most of us are lucky if we ever even took a class on children with special needs, and very few of us ever did any observation or internship in the special education area.

Another issue is the lack of support. Very few of us are fortunate enough to work in areas where we have the benefit of other professionals to support us in the classroom. Teachers cited a lack of administrative support and specialized training in strategies to work with students with ADHD as obstacles faced in their classroom (Guerra, Tiwan, Das, Vela, & Sharma, 2017). The reality is that as we have adopted the inclusion model, the training available to general education teachers has not been modified to teach us how to support students with ADHD. Additionally, the traditional supports such as paraprofessionals, smaller class sizes, modified curriculums, etc., found in a Special Education classroom are much less prevalent in general education classes.

I recall one of Jason's teachers in early elementary school who would not recommend Jason for gifted testing on the basis that there were other children with better behavior that were more deserving. She mentioned how other children consistently completed their work and showed effort in academics. Clearly, she did not view Jason's inability to complete work as an indication that he required more support in managing his ADHD but rather as a conduct issue. She spoke as if being gifted were some sort of reward or merit, missing the point that gifted children have very real needs to be addressed in their academic and intellectual development. I don't know if she couldn't understand that the behaviors associated with ADHD made the completion of assignments difficult or if she didn't accept or understand how being gifted and having ADHD could co-exist.

This anecdote illustrates how we tend to view children's needs for support through a lens of "good" or "bad" based on how their behaviors rate on an outdated scale of compliance. This paradigm certainly needs to shift since it does not allow us to clearly see our students' needs and ultimately undermines our ability to provide effective support. Teachers are in a position to do a lot of good, but they can also inadvertently do a lot of harm when they miss opportunities to support students.

I do not believe that many of Jason's teachers in general education have had the education and training necessary to meet my son's needs. Lawrence, Estrada, and McCormick's 2017 study showed that teachers' knowledge of how to support students with ADHD comes primarily from their own classroom experience, along with any personal experiences that they've had rather than from their teacher education. I never doubt the good intentions of educators; there is simply a lack of information and understanding. When adults in education are not adequately trained on how to deal with children with ADHD, children suffer the consequences. The self-esteem of the child, their social-emotional development, and their academic achievement are literally in the balance here. Jason is nine years old, and he already has some pretty bad scars from situations that were not well-managed.

THE INCLUSION MODEL & ADHD

Since my son's education is on the line here, as well as the education of millions of other kids, we need to be open and honest about this. Not only are many teachers not trained to support special needs, but also not all teachers are even comfortable teaching children with special needs. I do not mean this as a slur to teachers in any way. I am a Spanish teacher in a high school. I didn't realize the extent to which I would be involved in teaching kids with disabilities before I became a teacher. If I were to be really honest, my compassion for and understanding of ADHD happened as I experienced having a child with ADHD in the school system. I only became completely comfortable working with kids with ADHD after having Jason. The majority of general education teachers have not had the firsthand experience that could be gained through practicum with students with special needs during teacher education.

The challenge is that we are in the Inclusion Model, with all of its benefits and faults, and I'm a teacher, which means that my job is to educate the kids in my classroom. These children desperately need my help, and I was not trained to support them, but what CAN I do? That is the question that I must ask myself as a teacher.

Teaching children with ADHD under the best of circumstances is stressful, demanding, and at times even intimidating, particularly when students are unable to regulate their behavior and impulses. Teachers' self-efficacy and enjoyment of their profession are negatively affected by aggressive behavior directed toward them and others in the classroom (de Ruiter, Poorthuis, & Koomen, 2019). As teachers, we tend to disproportionately focus on externalized behaviors over internalized behaviors in students because of our lens of classroom management. Acting out, aggression, disruption, etc., cause issues within our classroom, threaten our control over the learning environment, and can cause harm to other students. We are, therefore, always on alert and more sensitive to externalized behaviors (Poorthuis & Koorem, 2019). This is why the kid with ADHD that is disruptive gets more attention than the child who also has ADHD but is inattentive.

Unfortunately, teacher shaming is real. None of us is an expert at everything or has infinite knowledge or patience. We all need support.

Education is a field that demands constant personal growth. As professionals, our "bedside manner" is perhaps the most crucial aspect of our practice. We are dealing with young people whose self-regulation and, in some cases, hormones, are all over the place. Many of our students are also carrying the additional burden of childhood trauma. As teachers, we are a parental figure and an authority figure. Our attitudes, or even perceived attitudes, towards a child can and do affect their self-esteem, beliefs about themselves, as well as if they consider themselves to be intelligent, adept at learning, and successful at school. Often as an educator, similarly to parenting, I am confronted with my own personal fears and limitations. To continue to be effective with children, I have to be willing to look at my preconceived notions, gaps of knowledge, and personal discomforts. Let's get started with this by debunking myths about ADHD and exploring strategies that will have you feeling more comfortable and supported as a teacher.

20 MYTHS DEBUNKED ABOUT ADHD

1. ADHD is a behavior problem controllable by the student.

ADHD is a neurological disorder. People are born with ADHD and have a deficiency of a neurotransmitter, norepinephrine, which is related to levels of dopamine. Neurotransmitter patterns are impaired in four different regions of the brain directly related to executive functions such as impulse control, self-regulation, transitioning from one activity to another, organization, focus, and hyperactivity. Through treatment plans that include behavior modification and classroom support, children can learn coping schools to improve, to varying degrees, in these areas (Blum et al., 2008).

2. Children with ADHD are lazy or do not put in enough effort.

Having ADHD has been described by many as having a brain that "never stops" or having an internal computer with hundreds of tabs open. Given this mental state, it requires a great deal of effort to focus in class. Sometimes students are either not able to maintain focus or, in many cases, feel worn out from the strain. Because focusing is difficult, there can be a natural resistance to tasks requiring sustained focus. This is where empathy and support can have a huge impact (Blum et al., 2008).

3. Kids with ADHD are incapable of focusing.

ADHD is really a disorder of attention, not a "deficit" of attention. In fact, a common symptom of ADHD is hyperfocus. This can be seen in the fact that children with ADHD more frequently have an "addiction" to screens. When they are in this mode, they easily lose track of time, perspective, and other responsibilities. It's not that children with ADHD aren't able to focus; it's more accurate to say that they are less able to regulate their attention span. Unfortunately, a lack of understanding of hyperfocus in children with ADHD has perpetuated the myth that their ability to focus is selective, not due to a neurological disorder (Porter, 2019).

4. All kids with ADHD are always hyperactive.

Some children with ADHD present as "hyperactive/impulsive" while others are "inattentive." Therefore it is very possible that a child is not hyperactive but distracted and still has ADHD. Also, no one is hyperactive every moment; there are times when people with ADHD have low levels of energy and prefer to be still. Jason basically has two extremes; he's either unable to sit still or he is calm, reflective, and very focused.

5. ADHD is more common in boys.

It's actually more like ADHD tends to be more obvious in boys. ADHD and ADD are both very common in girls and, in fact, under-diagnosed. Girls are more likely to present as inattentive than hyperactive. Unfortunately, since their symptoms are less visible, they are less likely to be diagnosed, which in many cases leads to higher negative outcomes later in life such as drug addiction, depression, bulimia, etc. (Ali, 2019).

6. ADHD is a learning disability.

Although approximately 30-50% of children with ADHD also have a learning disability, ADHD is not a learning disability. This point can cause confusion because often, the symptoms of ADHD can get in the way of learning. For example, a child that struggles with focus may find learning to read difficult; however, the child does not need support with decoding like a child with a reading disability would (Disabilities Association of America, 2020).

7. ADHD can be controlled by letting kids play outside more.

All children thrive with time to play outside. Play and physical activity offer numerous health benefits and social-emotional learning opportunities. That being said, although the hyperactivity associated with ADHD can be managed with movement, ADHD is a complex condition that requires multiple levels of support in several areas such as organization, self-regulation, and focus (Blum et al., 2008). Therefore although movement and time to play outdoors offer tremendous benefits, they do not cure a child of ADHD.

8. Kids outgrow ADHD.

Many adults struggle with ADHD. In many cases, this is exacerbated by not being adequately supported as children. We can support children with ADHD and help them to learn ways to manage their symptoms and to be more successful, but we must understand that ADHD is a lifelong neurological condition (Blum et al., 2008).

9. ADHD is a result of poor parenting.

It would be hard to find a parent of a child with ADHD who has not both been blamed and shamed by others, and questioned themselves about their own parenting; however, ADHD is a neurological condition that people are born with. There are strategies that encourage positive behavior, but all parenting strategies come with a learning curve.

10. ADHD is not a serious condition.

The first sentence of The Center for Disease Controls and Prevention (CDC) web review of ADHD is: "Attention-deficit/hyperactivity disorder (ADHD) is a serious public health problem." The article explores the effects on both the individual with ADHD and society as a whole (Center for Disease Control and Prevention, 2020). I daresay that a neurological condition that affects social relationships, emotional stability, self-esteem, and productivity from childhood to adulthood is rather serious.

11. All kids with ADHD have similar symptoms.

Children with ADHD experience a unique combination of the following symptoms: inattentiveness, impulsivity, and hyperactivity. Some children are either "hyperactive/impulsive" or "inattentive." There is also a large number of people with ADHD who have a comorbidity or concurrent condition such as Oppositional Defiant Disorder (ODD), a learning disability, sensory hypersensitivity, among others. Additionally, the symptoms of ADHD are affected by the environment, which varies throughout a child's day.

12. Medication is the recommended treatment for ADHD.

The Centers for Disease Control and Prevention recommends "Behavior therapy, including training for parents; and medications." As a teacher, I would like to add that classroom interventions are an integral part of the treatment for ADHD. ADHD has an often complex combination of symptoms that require a unique treatment plan for every child (Center for Disease Control and Prevention, 2020).

13. ADHD is an excuse.

ADHD is not an excuse for behavior—it is an explanation. Understanding ADHD provides us with insight and tools to address the challenging behavior that children with ADHD exhibit. The better we understand the condition, the better of a position we are in to support kids. When Jason was diagnosed with ADHD, it was empowering because I began to learn about his condition. Educating myself about ADHD was the beginning of being able to effectively support Jason.

14. ADHD is overdiagnosed.

ADHD diagnoses have increased in recent years as the awareness of the condition has increased, prompting some people to feel that every hyper child is now given a pill. In reality, ADHD is underdiagnosed, partly because arriving at a diagnosis occurs as a team effort between clinicians, parents, and educators. The diagnosis of ADHD is a complex process involving an observed behavior pattern consistent in at least two settings. There is no blood test; clinicians rely on observations and interviews, largely from educators and parents (Ginsberg, Quintero, Anand, Casillas, & Upadhyaya, 2014).

15. People with ADHD have trouble learning.

People with ADHD have trouble learning in the traditional classroom setting; however, overall, they are bright, creative, curious children. Jason is remarkably intellectual, often asking me questions about politics and philosophy and reading the news online independently. It takes a lot of support for him to complete assignments in school, however.

16. Kids that take ADHD meds are more likely to self-medicate with illegal drugs later on.

There is no evidence to support that children who take medication as part of their ADHD management plan have increased substance abuse later in life. In fact, a study accessed on the online US National

Library of Medicine, National Institute of Health showed that children whose ADHD symptoms are managed through medication have over a 31% less chance of abusing substances during early adulthood than their counterparts who were not on medication in childhood. Furthermore, it was shown that children whose ADHD was managed for a longer period through medication were increasingly less likely to abuse substances in adulthood (Chang et al., 2014).

17. ADHD can be controlled by limiting sugar consumption.

Most people, especially children, experience a burst of energy or hyperactivity when they consume high amounts of sugar. The "H" in "ADHD" is therefore affected by sugar consumption. While limiting sugar can affect a person's energy level, it will not cure a neurological disorder.

18. Kids with ADHD respond best to strict, authoritarian environments.

When Jason entered school, I thought that a school with a very traditional philosophy and authoritarian style would be best for him. In fact, I learned that the complete opposite is true; Jason needs to develop strong relationships with teachers; he does not respond well to authority without a solid foundation of mutual respect and connection.

19. People with ADHD are unconcerned about how their behavior affects others.

There have been a lot of studies on the relationship between ADHD and empathy. Being overstimulated can make it more difficult to view things from another's perspective. Impulsivity also plays a big role here; people with ADHD often act without considering the consequences of their actions for themselves or others. I have seen Jason cry many times because he hurt someone but say that when it was happening he was so mad that he couldn't stop himself.

20. ADHD is a new thing.

Hippocrates was discussing cases of children exhibiting ADHD symptoms over 2,000 years ago. ADHD is not a new disorder; however, like most mental health conditions, society has been slow to recognize, destigmatize, and effectively address ADHD.

STRATEGIES TO HANDLE CHALLENGES FACED BY TEACHERS

Learn about ADHD

You have my deepest respect for picking this book up. As a parent, you also have my heartfelt gratitude. Even though you went to a lot of school, you attend a lot of professional development, you have a demanding job, and have your own life, you have taken the time to seek to understand kids with ADHD. This is the all-important "step 1." Seeking knowledge about the condition will arm you with tools and strategies. There are numerous books, webinars, blogs, and other resources written from different perspectives available based on your needs and interests. Remember that your students are your greatest teachers. Observe them and, most importantly, notice not only their behavior but try to look past it to gain understanding about the "why." Talk to them, ask questions, show empathy—*learn together*. You will gain insight and positively impact their lives.

Become a Connected Educator

You are not limited to your own knowledge and resources. You are also not relegated to googling for answers to things that you don't know. You have access to experts in a variety of education and mental health fields. Educators have a large presence on social media. You can interact with other professionals with expertise in areas that you would like to learn more about easily by connecting on Twitter, Instagram, or Facebook. Twitter has scheduled chats under hashtags for almost any subject in education that you can imagine; they can be found by searching Twitter itself or Google. Blogs written by educators also offer common sense suggestions that are based on real-life rather than theory. These can also be found by using Google or a blog reader such as the one in WordPress. Most education authors have websites and are very accessible if you reach out to them. Don't be shy; educators on social media are passionate about their practice areas and have an online presence because they want to connect and share.

Join the #ADHDGlobalConvo and learn with educators and parents as we share resources and information to better support ADHD learners. You can join by following me on Twitter @BiscottiNicole or by following the hashtag #ADHDGlobalConvo. #ADHDGlobalConvo also has a group on Facebook. My website is updated with resources as well; you can visit or subscribe at nicolebiscotti.com

Strategic Differentiation

Differentiation can sometimes seem like a lofty goal or a buzzword that sets up unrealistic expectations for teachers. Delivering personalized learning for a large group of children matched to their individual learning preferences, needs, prior knowledge, and interests, while providing appropriate support is a tall order. At times implementing differentiation seems like an elusive ideal.

Class sizes can be large, and teachers are working within limitations based on a lack of adequate funding, meeting the needs of children who have experienced multiple forms of childhood trauma, language barriers, and more. All children, particularly those with special needs, often require specific supports that can be very challenging to identify and implement in large classrooms. While some students have Individualized Education Plans or 504's with detailed accommodations provided, numerous children with special needs have not been formally identified.

Fortunately, teaching is an art guided by science. Differentiation is powerful, research-based, and provides a framework to view how a lesson can be adapted to a group's needs. Carol Ann Tomlinson has written several books on the subject and identifies ways that teachers can differentiate: **content, process, and product**. There are key accommodations that can be applied universally to a class or a group that support the needs of ADHD learners while raising the quality of instruction overall.

- **Content** can be differentiated by inviting student choice (see chapter 5 for more about student choice) over topics within the framework and by offering differing levels of difficulty for a text. This allows students to engage and access information from where they are comfortable. Self-assessment tools such as short quizzes and rubrics can be helpful guides for students as they make choices about their learning.

- The **process** can be tailored to the interests of the student or a group of students within the constraints of the standards and curriculum by seeking ways to embed student choice. It can incorporate flexibility by allowing students to approach learning in a variety of different ways. Teachers can guide students by offering groups or stations that might choose a common approach. Grouping students by learning styles rather than ability provides a dynamic learning experience while offering the potential for higher engagement from individual group members. Teachers can scaffold this by guiding students in discovering their preferred learning styles and activities for learning.
- The **product** of learning, or the assessment, can be differentiated based on the student's needs and preferences by offering alternative assessment options, for example, such as a drawing, a poem, or creating a skit to demonstrate reading comprehension. This invites students to develop and showcase their own talents. When students share their unique projects, the teacher is no longer the sole keeper of knowledge, and students enjoy a rich peer learning experience that ultimately positively affects classroom culture.

The key to effective and realistic differentiation is to empower students to leverage differentiation for themselves. This implies that we begin to actively develop active learners. Rather than investing the great amount of time that we do in teaching compliance, we would shift to teaching the skills of self-advocacy and taking responsibility as a learner. We have to normalize students taking an active role in their learning and, for example, approaching us with an idea for an alternate assessment that we could then negotiate to ensure that it demonstrates mastery of the standard.

When we consider differentiation from the standpoint of whole-class accommodations that we encourage students to leverage, we can provide the opportunity for personalized learning to all students. The additional and powerful benefit to this approach is that we put decisions about learning in the hands of the learner, fostering independence, responsibility, and self-advocating. Rather than making assumptions about the learners' needs or holding meetings where the adults talk while the child sits there awkwardly, we begin to partner up with students and coach and encourage them to take an active role in their own learning. Today's students are not preparing for a world of uniformity; they are a part of a world of independent thinkers and innovators. Forming a learning community offers more to students than being a part of a classroom of passive learners.

REFLECTION POINTS

Let's continue this conversation and learn from one another. Share your thoughts in a tweet with the hashtag #ADHDGlobalConvo and feel free to mention me directly @BiscottiNicole.

- Does a lack of information about ADHD affect my practice as a teacher?
- What professional support can I find for myself?
- How can I embed opportunities for differentiation in my lessons?

RELATIONSHIPS - OPPORTUNITIES FOR IMPACT

POINTS TO PONDER

- How can I best support my students with ADHD?
- How can I find joy relating to my students with ADHD?
- How can I create a relationship with a student who seems angry and defiant?

∼

THE POWER OF STUDENT-TEACHER RELATIONSHIPS

"As far as I'm concerned hardly any teachers really understand me. When I was little I had a bunch of teachers who would get mad at me and I would just basically run around and act crazy. It pretty much would just get worse and worse. When I got a little bigger, I had a teacher that made me feel comfortable because when I would do something bad because I couldn't control myself she *wouldn't get super mad at me she would try to calm me down. If that didn't work then she would call the principal. She never seemed like she was mad at me though and she never made a big deal out of it when I came back, she just acted normal. Some of my other teachers got mad at me when I can't control myself and, like, just blamed me for it and they would also get super frustrated about it. But this teacher, I think like she understood that just happens sometimes to me and she didn't, like, get mad about it, she acted like it's a normal thing. And that helped me to calm down faster and then to not feel embarrassed or like the other kids don't like me when I would come back to the class. I really did feel like she knew how to deal with me because she was never, like, rude to me about it like the other teachers were."*

I'm a mother, but I can't switch off the teacher in me. Watching teachers, administrators, and other school personnel deal with Jason's behaviors has been one long and very insightful professional development. I have witnessed various education professionals with varying levels of experience and education handle Jason's behavior incidents. What stands out is how much the adult's mindset, training, ability to empathize, and compassion have directly impacted their and Jason's experience. I have seen the same child, even in the same classroom, respond very differently depending on which adult was working with him.

Positive relationships with students with ADHD have an impact on behavior, learning outcomes, and the long-term emotional and social well-being of the child that cannot be denied. As educators working with an at-risk population, we must be mindful of this potential benefit or harm to the child. When you develop a strong working relationship with a child with ADHD built on mutual trust, respect, and clear expectations, you are not only supporting that child in the short term, but you have a lifelong positive impact.

The student-teacher relationship is a foundational one in a child's life. Students form opinions about school and their ability to succeed in school largely based on their relationships with teachers. From a developmental standpoint, a child's school experience is generally their first experience navigating social roles and relationships independently, without family support. Teachers are ad hoc parental figures that provide an attachment-like relationship that affects a student's ability to cope with the demands of school, feel safe, and to develop social and academic confidence (Bergin & Bergin, 2009; Verschueren & Koomen 2012).

Because of the attachment-like aspect of teacher-student relationships, this relationship plays a significant role in student outcomes in terms of behavior, student achievement, and long-term well-being. This may seem intuitive to some degree, but it is all too often overlooked when we are stressed out, stretched, and unsure of how to relate to a student, particularly one with challenging behavior. Research shows us that children with positive relationships with teachers characterized by closeness and acceptance benefit from a "secure base" from which to explore and develop socially and academically. Teachers effectively become a safe haven for students, providing a sense of security and support with self-regulation. The result is enhanced social skills, better learning outcomes, and positive relationships with peers (Bergin & Bergin 2009; Koomen 2012; Pianta 1999; Verschuren & Koomen 2012, Zionts, 2005).

Unfortunately, the opposite effect can lead to a major downward spiral for Jason. When adults do not carefully construct a positive relationship with Jason, there is no limit to how badly things can end up. Once Jason perceives that an adult does not like him or is unfair to him, he loses all motivation to cooperate with them and becomes defensive. What we all expect as educators has been affirmed by research. Children not only misbehave more when they have teachers that they have a poor relationship with, but they are also more likely to misbehave intentionally (Al-Yagon & Mikulincer 2006; Silver et al., 2005).

Furthermore, the impact of a poor relationship with a teacher follows the student as they progress through school. I completely understand and acknowledge that Jason often gets into fights, is disruptive, and has overall challenging behavior; however, he relies on adults to support him with self-regulation because his disorder makes it difficult for him to do this alone. Poor and conflictive relationships between students and teachers have negative effects on children, such as higher rates of externalizing aggression, learning difficulties, and students withdrawing (Al-Yagon and Mikulincer 2006; Silver et al. 2005).

"If a teacher cares about me I will not get so angry all of the time and when I do get angry they can help me calm down. A lot of times I have teachers who I don't think understand me or are mean to me when I'm being bad. If they're rude to me when I'm mad I just get more mad. Sometimes when I'm mad about a problem at recess or something they just get mad at me for being mad. When I feel like teachers don't like me I start to not like them."

Your most powerful tool in managing challenging behaviors and supporting academic achievement is your relationship with the student. Research has shown that when children have a close relationship with their teacher, they exhibit less conflictive and aggressive behavior, higher motivation, and have better academic outcomes (Cavell, & Wilson, 2001; Furrer & Skinner, 2003; Hamre & Pianta, 2005; Hughes, Klem & Connell, 2004; Toste, Heath, & Dallaire, 2010).

Miss Jennifer, Jason's preschool teacher, shared the following: "There was a high turnover of teachers and frequent restructuring of classrooms, in addition to kids themselves coming and leaving. Often Jason's behavior seemed like it might be in response to these changes. It was apparent that he became anxious and craved proximity with a trusted adult at times. He always gravitated toward the older, more experienced teachers. He has said that they ask him less questions, seem more comfortable with him, and know what to do."

Miss Jennifer remembers that, "Jason often had incidents in which a power struggle would ensue between himself and an adult or he would become annoyed about another kid touching his building creations, or be uninterested in a direction given, or become annoyed with another child, and then become defiant, particularly if he felt that something was unfair. He always had the potential to become very angry very quickly. This would possibly escalate to hitting and kicking a person or object. Based on proximity, the target could have been furniture, a teacher, or a child. his source of annoyance, particularly whether it was the child who he felt got him in trouble or the adult that enforced a rule that he did not wish to comply."

Jason had frequent violent outbursts at nap time. Usually, Jason would get mad and get up and run around the classroom. The teachers would find themselves in hot pursuit of Jason around the room, and occasionally even outside. Jason says that he remembers very little of this, only that he was angry. I asked him what he was thinking about and he said that he was not focused; he was just running until the teacher caught him and would call me. Miss Jennifer pointed out that she took her break during nap time and was not in the room. She says that when she was in the room, Jason did not act this way. Although it happened frequently, she never witnessed it.

The adult who is around Jason during a moment of frustration has a lot of influence over how he will act. I can almost predict how far he will go around different teachers. Once he feels bonded with an adult, they will become a calming influence when he is upset. The opposite is also very true, particularly since he also has Oppositional Disorder. If he feels like the adult does not understand him, or worse, is mad at him, this seems to fuel him. Some teachers have been successful at calming him down and even avoiding these scenes altogether, and some have made them even worse. A good example of this is that Miss Jennifer doesn't recall ever witnessing one of Jason's scenes, although they frequently happened during preschool.

WHAT GETS IN THE WAY OF HAVING POSITIVE RELATIONSHIPS WITH OUR STUDENTS WITH ADHD?

One of the major problems that kids with ADHD are up against is that their condition is invisible. A key to successfully building relationships with kids with ADHD is viewing them through an accurate lens. They are often viewed as lazy, stubborn, disruptive, aggressive, and generally "bad." In fact, they suffer from an executive functioning disorder that makes self-regulation, social interactions, and focusing on tasks challenging. These just so happen to be some of the key skills that students need to be successful in school. For children with ADHD, school is generally a place that aggravates ADHD symptoms. The school setting, with its routines, high levels of stimulation, requirement of social skills, and emphasis on compliance is a source of struggle and therefore poor self-esteem and stigmatization, leaving students feeling frustrated, isolated, and with a negative self-concept (Brice, 1998; Carpenter & Austin 2008; Friio, 1999; Malacrida, 2001; McDannel, 2005; Prosser, 2006; Watson, 2011).

Be patient with me. Understand why I do the things I do.

Don't yell at me. Believe me, I don't want to have ADHD."

— *JOANE E RICHARDSON*

When we view children through a lens of misbehaving as opposed to having a neurological condition requiring support, we can't see the situation or the child's needs clearly. Not only do we make it difficult to adequately support them, but we also actually hurt them emotionally. Kids with ADHD are hungry for acceptance and connection. We can approach our kids with ADHD with impatience because of their difficulty behaving in class or we can approach them through the lens that they are trying hard with real barriers and need our support.

Frustration is easy to fall into, but unfortunately, very unproductive.

When Jason was smaller, he didn't really even understand why adults reacted negatively toward him. Jason's class was changed once when he was little because he had a teacher that was not a good fit for his needs and challenging behavior. After the change, and until the end of the school year, Jason would run to her class every day to give her a hug and then run to make line up for his after school program.

Another obstacle to creating impactful relationships is bias. We must check our own biases if we're serious about developing impactful relationships with kids with ADHD. It is very easy to typecast a kid like Jason. Teachers and administrators, while well-intentioned, are human. Jason often misbehaves, and it is very easy to begin to view him as a "problem kid." I have witnessed this happening many times.

Adults have even said things to him that were offensive and detrimental to his self-esteem.

Furthermore, they probably did not realize it while it was happening. Jason is pretty stoic in front of people he's not comfortable with, and he is also very private about his feelings. Many, many times, he has come home and asked to speak with me alone. We go into my room, and he will tell me about a comment that was made to him that offended him or hurt his feelings. In these conversations, he sometimes cries, is always exhausted after a difficult day, and needs me to listen and understand his point of view. As an adult, I can connect the dots, and I see what's going on. I try not to let on that the teacher or administrator might be making assumptions about him because of his behavior, but unfortunately, he already knows that.

My best illustration of the difference an adult's approach can make is an anecdote that I fondly refer to as "the tale of two principals." When Jason was small, we didn't understand what was going on or how to support him, and consequently, his world was filled with chaos. He acted out at school almost daily. The school that he attended had a traditional and even authoritarian approach, an approach that only served to exacerbate his Oppositional & Defiance Disorder. Jason's daily incidents culminated in a very regrettable episode where he was trying to run away from an administrator and found himself trapped and then inadvertently kicked the person. This incident initiated discussions about expulsion.

In his next school, I made it a point to proactively discuss the difficulties that Jason had at his prior school with the administration, hoping to avert another disaster. Jason did begin acting out after a short honeymoon period, and things got pretty messy from then on. The difference was that his principal seemed prepared for it. She didn't flinch when one day Jason ran out of the room and refused to come back. She personally chased him all over campus for over an hour.

There was also a time when she had to put him in a restraint. She never lost her composure. Sometimes Jason would yell awful things about hating her and the school. Even though Jason was on a variance, I watched her calmly tell my son that this was his school and that she was glad that he was there. She reassured both of us that we would work through this and find the right ways to support Jason. She also gave Jason appropriate consequences.

"I felt hyper in my classroom once and at this time I was in a new school. I felt, like, super hyper and then I just, like, want to get up and do something with my life because I'm, like, super bored and the teacher is just talking about shenanigans. I could not sit there anymore. I just got up and started running around the classroom and then out the door. I ran around the whole school. The principal finally caught me in the media center and held me down so I couldn't move. I felt sad when I got caught not because I got caught but just because, like, what I did it and all that. My mom came to the school to get me and I was just happy that my mom came at that point and I just started hugging her."

Within a couple of months of Jason attending this new school, something very unexpected happened. When Jason would become "spun up" and have to be removed, his teacher would call for an administrator, at which point Jason would sit in a designated seat in the hallway and calmly wait for the principal to arrive. Jason didn't negatively react to having the principal called because this was no longer a sign that he "was really in big trouble now." Sitting in his chair in the hallway and waiting for the principal was calming for him. He understood that he would have a consequence for his actions, but he also knew that she would talk with him, that she cared about him, and that perhaps most importantly, she understood him. I still marvel at the wisdom, patience, and persistence that it took for that person to build this level of rapport with him and of the incredible and lasting impact that relationship has had on him.

"At first I would run away if the teacher called the principal but then I realized the principal was really nice and I would be happy when she would call her because I would go to her office and she would talk to me and I would calm down and then I can return to my class. She knew how to calm me down like by talking to me and she knew that I liked to take walks and to help her and bring books back and forth to her office and my classroom at the library and do jobs like that and she never would get mad at me. I don't want to seem like I'm telling people what to do but I think that when children have trouble controlling themselves the best thing to do is what she did. It, like, helps them when you talk to them and take walks with them and give them jobs to do and definitely don't get mad at them because then it just hurts their feelings and makes them feel bad and they feel more pressure and then they just get in more trouble."

STRATEGIES

Your approach to children with ADHD makes all of the difference. I wish I could write that sentence ten times. Children with ADHD want to please you. Like any other child, they thrive on acceptance and praise. Unlike other children, they don't get a lot of acceptance and praise because they often are unable to conform to standard behavior expectations in the classroom. They become used to receiving negative feedback about themselves and their behavior. Most kids with ADHD spend a lot of time in trouble and hear repeated negative messages about themselves from adults. When you relate to them with the understanding that they are working with certain limitations and challenges, and show kindness, provide support, and above all, make them feel loved and accepted, it means the world to them.

Gaining Insight from Behavior

Behaviorism is one of the major constructs that helped me understand and become more effective with children with ADHD. Behaviorism teaches us about form and function, the way a behavior looks versus what purpose it serves. Every behavior has a form, which can be yelling, aggression, silence, etc. We have a tendency as humans to react emotionally to negative behaviors or to want to suppress them. Traditional school discipline is designed to suppress negative behaviors and to promote compliance. When we begin to question the function of behavior, we begin to really learn about children. This is powerful because, from this insight, we can begin to determine how to best meet kids' needs and to support them.

Behavior isn't something someone has. Rather, it emerges from the interaction of a person's biology, past experiences, and immediate context."

— L. TODD ROSE

I have found through the many phone calls about Jason I've received and my own experience as a teacher that one of the main reasons that kids with ADHD are underserved in school is their frequent displays of anger. Jason has certainly had his share of angry displays such as throwing things, running out of a classroom, hitting, and kicking, to name a few. Not all children with ADHD have anger issues, of course. ADHD presents in many different ways, so this may not apply to the experience you're having, but it's common and will serve well as an example of form versus function.

Children with ADHD suffer from a reduced ability to self-regulate as compared to most people. Most ADHDers are also impulsive and highly emotional. Given these characteristics of ADHD, it shouldn't be a shocker then when we are faced with a child who regularly and quickly displays explosive anger. Most of us are pretty uncomfortable with anger. We avoid it. We are afraid of it. We are expected to hide it because it's impolite. We reject people who display anger.

The behaviors associated with ADHD are not the problem; they are symptoms that can provide us with insight.

The problem is that our discomfort of anger gets in the way of our effectiveness. After ensuring students' safety, we are wise to begin to question the function of this behavior. Anger is rarely, if ever, a primary emotion but rather a cover of another emotion. Anger protects us, it helps us cope, and it gives us a sense of control when we feel most vulnerable. When we take this into consideration, we can view the scene where a child with ADHD just threw over a couple of chairs and is running out the door of the classroom in a different light. Perhaps we can begin to see children with ADHD's anger through a lens of form and function rather than reacting through our own discomfort and conditioning to suppress anger. We could begin by seeking to understand the function of the behaviors to understand what is underneath the anger. Is the child afraid, overwhelmed, anxious, scared, bored?

"I remember I was at my preschool and I was mad, I think because I just wanted to play with legos but some other kid kept saying 'no.' I grabbed a big ruler and just started hitting everything I could see. I was about to explode and I was running and the teachers were chasing me. It's not like I wanted to do that or it's not like this was my

way to get my anger out. I was just so angry I didn't even know what I was doing and at that point I was just still mad at the kid."

Educators that are successful with students with ADHD show compassion and truly understand that for children with ADHD, school is generally a huge struggle. Empathy is definitely the secret sauce with ADHD. Most of these children have been struggling to behave in a way that is imposed on them, not natural to them, and not always possible, and are punished frequently for failing. Most people just do not understand why it is so frustrating to be in a room full of kids that are moving and frequently talking and have to focus on something that you're not interested in while being triggered by several things in your environment and frequent, fast thoughts going through your mind (Brice, 1998; Carpenter & Austin, 2008; Friio, 1999; Malacrida, 2001; McDannel, 2005; Prosser, 2006; Watson, 2011).

This is a great example of why teachers, parents, and kids have to work together and develop strong communication to support children with ADHD. Supporting kids with ADHD is so much more a conversation than a list of strategies. Most of the time, they don't even immediately know why they are reacting to something so strongly. Helping them to work through their emotions and to identify triggers is an integral part of learning to cope. Children with ADHD need support in calming down and working through anger, much like we all do at times.

Modeling through Interactions

The quality of a teacher's interactions with kids have a documented impact on their social-emotional and academic achievement. A teacher's ability to provide supportive interactions is not correlated to their academic background nor their years of experience but rather to their own ability to provide emotional support to children. Teachers teach behavior through modeling. An example of this is the tendency to raise one's voice when kids are being loud. It's actually more effective to speak quietly so that students have to adjust their noise level to hear you. They also set the tone for teacher-student interactions in three key areas: emotional support, organization of the learning environment, and support for instruction. Teachers support student achievement, self-regulation, and positive social skills through their own interactions with children (Williford, Maier, Downer, Pianta, & Howes, 2013).

A few traits stand out about educators that are effective with kids with ADHD. First of all, they are looking at kids with ADHD through a fair lens. They know enough about the condition to have reasonable expectations and are not shocked by the challenging behavior that often presents with ADHD. Second, they do not take anything personally. Again, they understand that kids with ADHD will often react quickly and tend to act out. This does not make them angry or frustrated. They are calm and confident, at least on the exterior. This is extremely effective because when kids are in emotional turmoil and struggling to self-regulate, the last thing that they need is for the adults to be out of control as well. I have found as a teacher that kids with ADHD will generally go above and beyond for you when they perceive your acceptance and support.

Positive Reinforcement

Schools and districts have a variety of different behavior management systems that are largely built on positive reinforcement. Some schools use Positive Behavior Intervention Supports (PBIS), some use (RTI), among other popular programs. There are some common threads, such as an emphasis on communicating clear expectations and recognizing and rewarding positive behavior. These programs have a lot to offer to children with ADHD.

Students with ADHD often find themselves in a vicious cycle of misbehavior because of their ADHD symptoms compounded by feelings of stress and frustration from receiving punitive measures and negative feedback, which leads to a feeling of being judged unfairly by teachers, thus creating a situation in which they approach a new teacher in a defensive stance. While children are struggling to be able to focus and to pay attention, they are frequently shamed and punished. These children have feelings and are internalizing negative and hurtful messages about themselves. I have seen this time and time again with my son, particularly as he matures and becomes more aware. Sometimes he implodes and feels badly about himself, and other times, he explodes and acts out. As educators, we cannot forget that children's' self-esteem, feelings of self-efficacy, attitudes toward school, and ability to trust adults are at stake here (Friio 1999; Hands, 2010; Hibbitts,2010; Hougton et al., 2006; Hughes, 2007; Prosser, 2006; Singh, 2011).

Positive reinforcement provides multiple benefits that children with ADHD specifically need. Let's start with the word "positive." Kids with ADHD receive an inordinate amount of negative feedback throughout their lives. Focusing on the positive gives them a chance to "win," even if the wins are initially small. Consider the difference between asking a kid to sit still during silent reading time and praising them for being still so far and asking them to continue. Teachers can use acknowledging these small wins to convey empathy for them and to communicate they are in the child's corner. Both of these outcomes are relationship builders.

There are a variety of token reward systems related to positive reinforcement programs. Acknowledge in any form is a great reminder and motivator. I had a student who started the year by ditching almost every day. A few times, I asked another student to text him and ask him to come to class because he was missed. When he would show up, I always told him how happy I was to see him. He would smile back and tell me that he came because I would "track him down" if he didn't. I later found out that most days he only attended my class, which ironically was in the middle of the day. Kids enjoy getting prizes; however never underestimate the impact of verbal praise and of acknowledging them. As cool as stuff from a prize box is, what leaves a lasting impression on us is how others make us feel about ourselves. Interestingly what doesn't cost money has the most return on investment.

REFLECTION POINTS

Let's continue this conversation and learn from one another. Share your thoughts in a tweet with the hashtag #ADHDGlobalConvo and feel free to mention me directly @BiscottiNicole.

- What obstacles might I have in relating to students with ADHD?
- What strategies can I use to improve my relationships with students with ADHD?
- How can my positive relationships with students with ADHD impact my whole class?

ADHDERS RAISE THE BAR FOR EVERYONE

POINTS TO PONDER

- How can I accommodate the needs of my students with ADHD while meeting the needs of all children?
- How should my lessons be designed to maximize learning outcomes for kids with ADHD?
- What are the learning activities that most engage students with ADHD?
- Which assessments are the most fair and accurate for students with ADHD?

Rather than addressing separate strategies for the ADHD learner, this book presents whole-class strategies that increase learning for all while addressing the needs of the ADHD learner. I believe that considering the needs of the ADHD learner when designing lessons and classroom culture challenges the teacher to create a higher quality learning environment that benefits everyone and proactively addresses some of the challenges of ADHD learners. I have found that if I plan my classroom instruction to accommodate my ADHD learners, there's a great chance that I'll hit a home run in terms of my students' engagement. Rather than viewing them as outliers, my students with ADHD have become my litmus test for a boring lesson. My other students might politely suffer through it when I'm having an off day, but my ADHDers not so much. Embracing this continues to be a growth opportunity for me as a teacher and pushes me to improve the quality of my instructional design. Jason's requests for support are shared to provide the perspective of a child with ADHD; however, the strategies presented in this book are designed to benefit all learners.

What if our ADHDers can show us new ways of teaching and learning that raise engagement and achievement for everyone?

5 Practice Strategies for Students with ADHD

01 Pace
Keep lessons and practice fast paced. Have more activities planned than you think you'll need.

02 Movement
Moving actually helps ADHD brains concentrate better! Build in movement & allow it to happen when needed.

03 Novelty
Newness = interest. Keep incorporating new or surprising ideas into each session.

04 Focal Point
Use physical items, sticky notes, and dots on fingers as a few examples.

05 Structure
Help to structure practice - don't leave it up to them.

Printed with permission by Christine Gooder, Director: Oregon Suzuki Institute

A CLASSROOM CULTURE OF SUPPORT

An investment in creating a culture of communication and support offers benefits to all students. Encouraging students to get to know one another and to share their experiences, knowledge, and perspectives provides for a rich learning environment and fosters acceptance. Children with ADHD offer multiple strengths to their classroom community, both socially and academically. A classroom culture that encourages students to share their perspectives, to respect one another, and values that the teacher as not the only "knower of knowledge" opens the space for students to become more supportive of one another. There have been countless times that I noticed that another student was able to explain a concept to his or her peer more effectively than I was. Those exchanges should be celebrated as they embody a learning community (Moore, Russell, Arnell, & Ford, 2017).

One of the greatest paradoxes of being a teacher is the very real need to provide individualized support to an entire classroom of children. There are universal supports that can become a part of every classroom that support all children. All kids need support, whether they have special needs or not. Support is not help, and it's not enabling. Peg Grafwallner explains the concept of "capable support" in her article, "What is Capable Support?" which was published in the ASCD's blog in 2017. Below are excerpts of this article; however,— I highly recommend reading the article in its entirety. It changed my perspective forever.

I am an Instructional Coach and Reading Specialist at a large urban high school.

I am also Ani's mom...

...As a parent of a Special Needs child and as a teacher in a large urban school district, I have a unique perspective. I see many parents who "help" their children and as a result, they do their children a great disservice. They immediately fly into the "I don't want to see you suffer, so I will gladly do this for you" (because sometimes that's what "help" looks like) mode every time they smell calamity or perceive that things have become too "hard." Heaven forbid life gets tough.

Instead of helping, let's focus on support. There is a difference.

What does help look like and what does support look like when we are talking about my Ani or perhaps, other special education students?

It looks like it does for any other kid...

...Support her as you would support any other child. Don't do it for her and don't feel sorry for her. She might surprise you. Ani's way works for her. It might take time and you might do it differently. But that has to be okay. Finally, remember even though she might be labeled "special needs," she is as special as any other child—with all the manipulative behavior that all of us own...

The term "supports" in the context of the special needs child can refer to accommodations and modifications writing into an IEP or Plan 504. It can also refer to an infinite number of resources or strategies used to encourage social and academic success. Supports are put into place to mitigate the negative effects of the child's disability. For example, a child with sensory hyperactivity could be more comfortable and therefore attentive if they were allowed to use noise-canceling headphones.

Although we tend to refer to supports that are specific to the child with a disability, their success can also be positively impacted by others receiving support as well. Teachers benefit from professional learning, conferences, mentors, and other resources. Students in the classroom who do not have special needs also need support to understand ADHD and for the added stress that can be placed on them when children with ADHD are disruptive to the learning environment. Placing strategic and effective supports in the classroom in multiple layers not only benefits children with ADHD but also improves the entire learning community's success.

Jason's requests for support are, of course, unique to his individual needs; however, I've included them as some may apply to other students with ADHD. Having a conversation about support to write this section in and of itself was very informative for me. Even though I'm familiar with Jason's needs and preferences, writing and then reading this was an opportunity for reflection. When we ask kids what they need, we empower them by promoting self-advocacy skills, and sometimes we can see where we were falling into assumptions or imposing our own learning needs onto another person. Conversations about support can take place in low-pressure ways such as through surveys and conferences.

Children with ADHD are so used to being punished for their behavior that they are generally thrilled to be asked what they need.

THE HELP I WANT BY JASON

To Sit in a Quiet Place

"I don't want to bother anyone but I like to sit in a place where it's quieter and not that much like going on around me. It's ok if I'm in the back or kind of by myself because I'm more comfortable if I can focus better and also I make a lot of noise and I don't want to bother other people. When there's too much noise around me I either get mad or I get distracted and start messing around so it's better to just let me sit alone and then I kind of don't have those problems as much. I know I can be pretty annoying because I move a lot and with the noise thing too so it's probably better for others kids honestly too. I know I can distract other kids a lot."

"Sometimes it helps me to function and to do my work to sit by my teacher because sometimes it feels like I'm just like in some other world and I don't know what to do so when she's near me it reminds me of what to do. I prefer to sit, like, at a table with her because I think I do my work better. When I'm distracted I like for her to allow me to come sit by her also because it's quieter and that helps me a lot. I like to be able to go work at her table if I need to but I have to be truthful and say that I don't like if teachers get close to me too much all the time if I don't feel comfortable with them because sometimes it makes me feel, like, a little awkward. I like it better when they let me go over to them when I need to be next to them."

Help to Follow the Rules

Most resources and guidelines for working with kids with ADHD suggest that teachers should constantly remind students with ADHD about the classroom rules and that we should be explicit in explaining the purpose of the rules. I've even seen guidance that we should be posting notes to their desks or posting the rules where it is in close proximity to them so that they can better remember them. From conversations with Jason, I have learned that it is much more complex than a problem of understanding or remembering the rule. There are two parts here: one being that the child with ADHD knows and understands the rule but struggles with the self-regulation necessary to consistently follow the rules, and the other being that children with ADHD have difficulty with multiple directives at once because of their lack of focus. The first would be that a child understands the rule but gets easily caught up in emotion and acts impulsively; the second would present as a child being told to follow a series of steps and becoming overwhelmed.

"A lot of teachers keep reminding me of the rules and telling me stuff like how I hurt someone or am doing things that are bad for the classroom community. I already understand the rules and already feel sad when I hurt someone. Actually when they just keep repeating it I feel even more sad and embarrassed. I don't mean to sound rude or something but I already know that. I would rather the teacher just remind me to calm down or give me a chance to calm myself down. That's actually the problem, I get so mad and frustrated and then it's really hard to follow the rules when I feel like that all at once."

Essentially what Jason is expressing is a need for support with self-regulation. In the heat of the moment, his impulsivity takes over, and he does not even think about the rules or the consequences for himself or others. This is very different from not understanding the consequences or forgetting the rules. The most effective way to reduce these situations is to have a strong working relationship with the student and to have supports in place for when they are unable to self-regulate. These situations will arise, and it's best to have action plans established. For example, when Jason becomes overwhelmed, he makes a sign to the teacher and leaves to go to a designated area.

The most effective way to implement support for self-regulation is both universally and individually. People often reference young children in conversations about self-regulation, but I teach high school and certainly have seen my share of students struggling with self-regulation. In reality, we all could use a little support in this area from time to time. By proactively having this support as an integral part of our classroom community, we create an enhanced learning environment that is supportive to everyone.

When working with individual children, co-regulation plays an important role as we must model calm for our students. We're humans also and can be stressed or tired and find ourselves reacting emotionally. If we apply Vygotsky's construct of learning through socialization, children are constantly learning from our behavior and how we react to situations. Once we calm ourselves, we can assist children with co-regulating. Kids need the support of a trusted adult to become calm themselves. If they perceive that the adult is angry, impatient, disapproving, etc., they will continue to maintain a tense state in reaction. Co-regulation not only helps kids in the short term, but it is also effective in the long term as it supports children in developing a lifelong skill. It is much less about telling them what is right and wrong and much more about letting them find calm. When they are centered, most children can quickly distinguish between positive and negative behaviors. Children do not need to be coerced or threatened into calming down; they need the adult to provide a landing pad when they are running high on emotions. Once the child has calmed down, collaborative problem solving can begin.

Directions I Can Remember

"I can't understand a bunch of instructions at a time. Sometimes I don't remember or understand one. When people tell me a lot of things to do at once, I don't know where to start, it all just sounds like blah, blah, blah in my head. Don't get me wrong, I want to do them, I just feel, like, overwhelmed. I need teachers to understand that I am trying to do them even though sometimes it looks like I'm not because I get distracted and start doing something else. Just like remind me and then I'll focus and that helps me get back on track. I always have a lot of random stuff in my head so it makes it hard to do everything someone's telling me to do."

All kids need clear expectations and directions. Kids with ADHD usually need them one at a time. Not necessarily repeated, just not all at once. It is very hard for them to focus and to be present enough to remember multiple steps. Because this is so hard for them, they can tend to either become angry or to give up. Countless classroom-wide strategies can support kids in remembering multiple steps or tasks. Writing them on the board is great, as is posting them to a common online space or platform. Some teachers prefer to give handouts. This works for some kids, but for others who struggle with organization, it might become one more thing to add to the pile in their backpack or to lose. Depending on the circumstances, it can be a great investment of time to have kids write down the steps for their own reference. In some cases, it's most effective for the teacher to provide the steps and allow the student to copy them in a lower pressure situation than during instruction. Some people remember things better when they write them themselves, and it encourages students to take responsibility for their schoolwork by creating their own reminder.

"I think if teachers wouldn't make such confusing statements it would be easier for me. Like maybe write it on a paper or let me do it alone."

For children with ADHD, there are many individual supports that teachers can provide to help them with remembering multiple items. Teachers can help kids to create an organization system or provide directions step-by-step individually as each step is completed. The ideas are endless, but the guiding principles here are that the supports should be developed *collaboratively* with the student, be measurably effective, and progress toward the student developing better organization skills.

Help Me Learn about Stuff I'm Interested in

"I am very interested in a lot of things and want to learn and be smart. I wish I could learn about things that I'm interested in and already curious about. I ask my mom a lot of questions and we watch videos together about all kinds of random stuff like volcanoes, Martin Luther King, the planets, the Pilgrims, and a lot of things. I also really like to build stuff and to figure out how things work. I wish my mom could homeschool me so that I could learn more because I feel like school is repeatedly Math, Writing, and Reading. I know that's important but I want to learn about things too."

In *Mindful Education for ADHD Students,* experts Victoria Proulx-Schirduan and C. Branton Shearer remind us of the many strengths that are part of the profile of a child with an attention disorder, including keen spatial intelligence, creativity, and "naturalist intelligence," or understanding of the outside world. All too often, these strengths are drowned out by the more traditional demands of the school environment: speaking softly and sitting still. A child with

ADD, however, may not only thrive working in your school garden but lead other children in caring for it. Teachers agree it takes time to uncover the strengths of all students, not just those with attention disorders.

Learning what your students' interests are is the first step to having a class full of engaged learners. When you spend a few minutes speaking to students individually, you get to know them and build rapport. With our kids with ADHD, this rapport is crucial because it is an investment of time and caring that will pay off during difficult situations or when tensions are high. I encourage you to find partnership strategies and opportunities that are well suited for you and your classroom. The possibilities are endless. If you have a strategy or strategies that you are already successfully using or find one that you would like to share, please tweet about it with the hashtag #ADHD-GlobalConvo.

FORM VS. FUNCTION IN TERMS OF SUPPORTS FOR LEARNING

Having ADHD is exhausting, frustrating, scary, and overwhelming. When Jason has a "bad" day, he comes home upset, tired, and drained. He'll often tell me that he wants for us to talk alone or that he wants me to watch a show with him. He almost always ends up snuggling up to me and falling asleep. When we see a kid displaying the kind of challenging and frustrating behavior that Jason displays, we often don't realize that the kid is actually frustrated and exhausted as well. Now add disappointment in himself. He needs support; school is a struggle for Jason.

If we refer to Applied Behavior Theory, we realize that behavior takes different "forms" but always serves a "function." When teachers understand and apply this concept, they are more successful at avoiding larger disruptions in the classroom by understanding kids' needs and being responsive (Young, Andres, Hayes, & Valdez, 2018). A child who acts up every day during math might be avoiding the lesson because it is difficult for them to concentrate that long or to process and remember multiple steps. Another student who talks nonstop during reading class may want to seek the attention of others to ease their anxiety about difficulty reading.

"If the teacher looks at me during math time she will probably see me getting up out of my chair, not doing the work, or stomping all of the time. When we have math time I can't focus and then I get mad so I don't end up doing my work. I really like math but how they explain it just hurts my head. There are too many steps and then I get confused."

We have to look past the "form" of the behavior to learn about the "function." When we do this, we can begin to effectively address the obstacles to learning and have a real impact. This is an area that has a large return on investment of our efforts. When we spend a little time observing and asking "why," we are able to adequately address the needs of the child rather than throwing a bunch of interventions their way and hoping one will work. Knowing the function of behavior in relationship to learning gives us the insight we need and avoids frustration for the child and the teacher.

COMPLIANCE DOES NOT EQUAL LEARNING

Expect more than compliance; expect learning and achievement. We all have an idealistic image of how our classroom should run and how our students should behave. In many cases, this is not the reality in our classrooms. Classroom management issues should all be viewed through one lens—what is conducive for teaching and learning. It is our responsibility to create and maintain a positive learning environment.

Think of a classroom where teaching and learning are happening. It may help to ask colleagues if you can observe their classes. What does a productive class look like? What does it sound like? What is the body language of the students? The teacher? What does the environment feel like? After you've created this image in your mind, think of what rules and procedures will support you in creating this reality. Remember, it's less important to be attached to your preferences than to create a true learning environment. Decide what expectations you will need to be very firm on and which you can give the kids some freedom with.

You may observe a class where the students are louder than you would have expected or where they are using their phones. Decide where you can give up control without compromising the learning environment. I find that by making a few concessions, I receive more cooperation from students in general. At its core, teaching and learning is a give-and-take relationship.

We are largely biased against kids with ADHD because many of us were taught to value compliance.

"Sometimes I feel like my teacher wants to control me and we're not really learning, just doing what they say. I want to have a choice about what I'm learning and my assignments and learn things that I'm interested in. I'm interested in lots of stuff but how they do it just makes it boring and makes me not want to do it. I feel like teachers aren't supposed to be like the CEO of a robot factory and just want kids to do what they say."

Kids with ADHD can easily (and often) take over a classroom and monopolize the teacher's attention. They can also be a focal point for the other students as well because their behavior definitely grabs attention. It is very easy to fall into the idea that if a child with ADHD is "behaving," they are doing well. Remember, *compliance does not equal learning*. Students with ADHD may stop exhibiting disruptive behavior for various reasons; however, we must still be vigilant to ensure that the child is working to their potential.

REFLECTION POINTS

Let's continue this conversation and learn from one another. Share your thoughts in a tweet with the hashtag #ADHDGlobalConvo and feel free to mention me directly @BiscottiNicole.

- What is my definition of support in a classroom?
- Do I think that some of your students might feel the same way about support? Why or why not?
- How can I use my understanding of form versus function to provide meaningful support for my students?

WHOLE-CLASS STRATEGIES THAT ADDRESS THE NEEDS OF CHILDREN WITH ADHD

 It is difficult to instruct children because of their natural inattention; the true mode, of course, is to first make our modes interesting to them."

— *JOHN LOCKE*

DEVELOPING AN ACADEMIC MINDSET

Children with ADHD struggle with executive function tasks such as organization, planning, goal setting, sustained focus, and maintaining motivation. These are skills that not only increase academic achievement but are part of our long-term personal growth. Perhaps most importantly, we know that not all of our students come to us with a background with a focus that emphasizes developing a mindset for academic success; however, we do know that this is a strong indicator of students' success. We do not learn these skills once, but continually grow in these areas on a continuum. When we embed these skills into our classroom culture, we proactively support all kids' academic achievement.

Dr. Kevin Leichtman, Director of Academic Mindset, provides strategies that benefit all students while targeting the needs of students with ADHD,

> Whole class interventions can be a particularly effective way to benefit students with ADHD while also advancing the objectives of the entire class. Often, students with exceptionalities are given separate interventions that focus on deficiencies, areas of need, limiting factors, etc. I have often received messages about students with ADHD, stating, 'I know he can't do this, but…' or 'She isn't good enough at…' and many other phrases along those lines. These deficiency-focused messages do not just harm the curricular success of students, but they can also play a role in limiting their executive functioning skills.
>
> By providing whole class interventions on executive functioning, it is possible to provide an asset-based approach to building all of your students' skills in a setting where ADHD students are not singled out, isolated, or limited by deficiency language. Better yet, your whole class will benefit from the development of these soft skills as they apply it to their classroom behaviors and performances.
>
> At Academic Mindset, we focus on skills that promote success in every aspect of life, which is important for all students but vital for ADHD students who may be focused on deficit talk

and what others perceive as their limitations. Some examples of this skill work include:

- Setting goals and creating specific action plans designed to reach those goals
- Building intrinsic motivation by creating support systems and identifying role models
- Mapping out habits and routines that allow students to perform at their highest levels with more consistency
- Identifying strengths and utilizing them as a source of confidence to overcome perceived weaknesses.

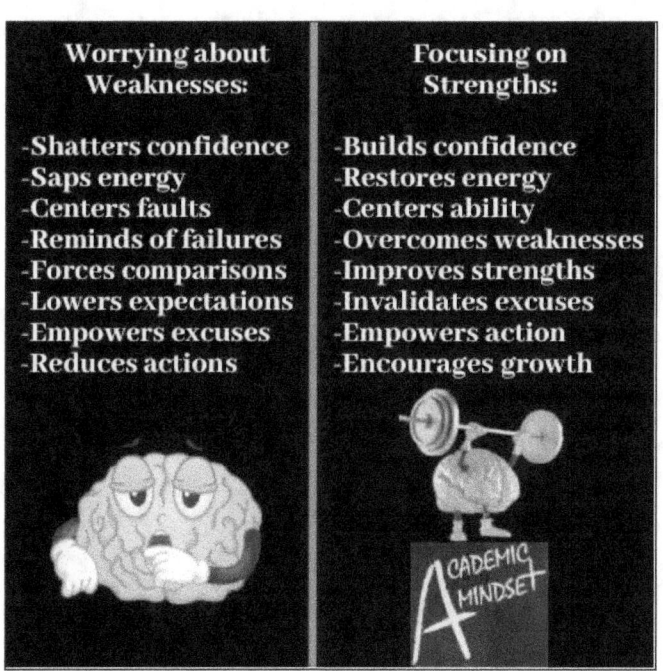

Printed with permission from Academic Mindset.

In my experience as a teacher and a mother, I have found that most children need a supportive framework to be organized. When I take the time to teach organization strategies, I am delighted at the results. The reverse is true; when I assume that kids should know how to be organized, I am disappointed and, in all honesty, have not set them up for success. Organization is a difficult skill for ADHDers, but actually, very few people are born with excellent organization skills; most people learn them.

Organization can be explicitly and implicitly taught. One of the most important things that we can do as teachers is to model organization and to extend this through the classroom procedures that we put into place. Our classroom procedures provide the "how" of organization for many of our students. Even at the high school level, explicitly teaching organization as we progress on projects alleviates a lot of stress in my students and provides them with tools they can continue to use.

Embedding goal setting is powerful for everyone in the class. During group and individual projects, after sharing the guidelines and rubric, I ask students to create daily goals. One year I wrote three of my goals in the corner of my whiteboard and asked the students to take five minutes to write down three goals that they had for themselves during the semester. I left the sharing of the goals optional. The supportive conversations that came out of this five-minute exercise really touched my teacher's heart. For the rest of the year, students would ask me about my progress toward my goals. When I shared honestly, they would often comment on their own progress, even sparking positive and supportive conversations between them.

Specific Benefits to Children with ADHD

Organization, planning, positive mindset

REFLECTION POINTS

Let's continue this conversation and learn from one another. Share your thoughts in a tweet with the hashtag #ADHDGlobalConvo and feel free to mention me directly @BiscottiNicole.

- How can I embed activities to promote a positive mindset that my class would enjoy?
- What procedures can I include in my classroom to encourage students to be organized?
- In what ways can I encourage support systems to become a part of our classroom culture?

STUDENT CHOICE & VOICE

Implementing student choice helps you learn about your students.

"I wish I could choose some certain activities because some activities are confusing or boring to me. If I'm interested in something I want to focus on it and have time to get involved with it. I don't like when we change activities a lot during the day. It's like I either get super interested in something and want to just focus all of my energy on it or I am bored and have trouble focusing. I think if I could choose some of the things that I did, I could find stuff that I really like and want to learn about and not feel bored and frustrated. Also then I would learn

better and behave better because everything wouldn't seem like just I don't know what we're doing and why we're doing it. Sometimes I can really get into stuff and learn a lot, trust me, I'm not all that bad, I can really focus. I'm kind of making a joke here but I'm actually pretty serious at the same time."

Barbara Bray, Creative Learning Strategist, Podcast Host, and Author of *Define Your WHY,* shares,

> Voice gives students a chance to share their opinions about something they believe in. There are so many aspects of "school" and "learning" where students have not been given the opportunity to be active participants. Some students, especially those that are concerned about extrinsic factors like grades, may not feel comfortable expressing their own opinions. Giving students voice encourages them to participate in and eventually to own and drive their learning. This means a complete shift from the traditional approach of teaching compliance that develops a 'learned helplessness' to encouraging voice where there is authenticity in the learning.

WHOLE-CLASS STRATEGIES THAT ADDRESS THE NEEDS OF CHILDREN WITH ADHD

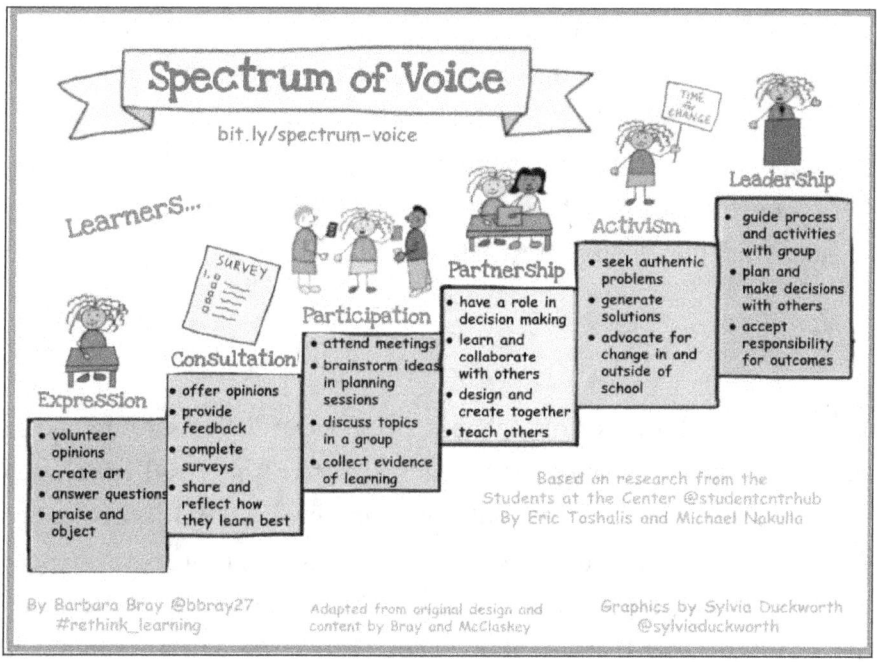

The goal of providing more choice is to move from being participants of learning to become self-directed, independent learners with agency. It is about teachers and learners changing mindsets and having "can do" attitudes. This takes time and a process for both teachers and learners. When you acquire the skills needed for advocacy and innovation, students automatically take more responsibility for their learning. The more choices students make on their own will give them the skills to advocate for what they are passionate about and become more innovative about how they discover their purpose for learning.

The idea of 'school' is supposed to be about building relationships with teachers and students that develop into a culture of learning. If you ask students with ADHD about something they are interested in, you open doors to discussions they want to have. Encouraging voice and providing opportunities for choice demonstrates that teachers care about them. When teachers engage in meaningful conversations based on authentic issues and personal interests, then students feel empowered to share their ideas and make decisions on how and what they learn (Bray, 2020) .

Jason has spent a lot of his school career out of the classroom and in trouble. Ironically, Jason spends as much free time as I have each evening learning. He is very interested in politics, civil rights issues, science, architecture, the environment, math properties, and gender equality, among other areas of interest. I'm a teacher, so I know that the luxury of time that I have to spend with Jason and his siblings is not relevant or realistic in terms of a discussion on the classroom setting where teachers have to cover curriculum and meet the needs of 30-40 kids at the same time. The question, though, remains: "How can we support a love of learning in kids who have a really hard time coping in the classroom environment?"

When you allow student choice and voice in your classroom, you invite students to be active rather than passive learners. Kids are curious about so many things, and when we become curious about what their interests are, we learn about our students. Perhaps, surprisingly, we also learn from our students. Sharing is the foundation of a learning community. Teachers have to teach standards, but we can approach the standards in many different ways. When we give students choices about how they demonstrate their knowledge or over the topic of their project, we increase engagement, community, and learning.

. . .

Specific Benefits to Children with ADHD

Engagement, diverse talents

REFLECTION POINTS

Let's continue this conversation and learn from one another. Share your thoughts in a tweet and use the hashtag #ADHDGlobalConvo and feel free to mention me directly @BiscottiNicole.

1. How can I embed organizational and other academic skills into my activities and overall classroom culture?
2. Within my curriculum and lesson design, where can I embed opportunities for student choice or topics and or activities?
3. What are options for activities that I can provide that would be effective assessments of knowledge?

ENCOURAGING DIVERSE TALENTS

I teach Spanish, and one of the greatest joys that I've had as a teacher is to see kids who are normally not very engaged light up when they are given permission to let their talents shine. One year I had a student who was very pleasant but disengaged bring down the house with his knowledge of norteño music and ability to sing and play the accordion during a cultural project. The whole class and I learned a great deal about his heritage and about him as a person from that activity.

Another student who rarely turned in assignments really impressed me with his reading comprehension when I allowed him to make a poster rather than write an essay as a book reflection. This young man had tremendous artistic talent but wasn't a confident writer. His poster reflected great effort, attention to detail, and most importantly, showed that he was able to analyze the book very well. One of the competencies for Spanish is writing, but allowing this student to use his talent to demonstrate his comprehension of the book laid the foundation for me to support him more effectively when he wrote.

Kate Lindquist, M.Ed., and Art Teacher, shares strategies about incorporating the opportunity for students to explore their own talents in the classroom.

> When working with children specifically with ADD/ADHD, know that they have the potential to soar. It's just that their potential is scattered in a million directions and brain waves keep blowing them all around. Their potential lies in their intelligence, creativity, spontaneity, and ability to hyper-focus (on a topic of interest), all of which are common characteristics found in people with ADD/ADHD. These assets are often overlooked because disruptive behaviors take the stage. Due to the fact that most lessons are fairly restrictive in nature, the opportunity for these students to shine is often lost. As an arts educator, I have seen that allowing a child with ADD/ADHD a little more wiggle room can work wonders. They still complete the project in its entirety but with a few accommodations…maybe they use paint instead of markers, or draw and label a car instead of a robot, or complete just the rough sketch of my lesson but include a song or dance as the rest.

This leads me to share a magic secret...The arts can be a powerful tool in your back pocket when working with not just learners with ADD/ADHD but ALL learners. Art, music, and movement art an innate language within us all. Before we know the meaning of words or how even how to speak, we are able to express ourselves through the arts. Crying might not be the most melodious sound at 2 am, but it's a newborn's musical communication. The colorful animals swirling on a mobile above a crib mesmerize a child and calm them down. Even animals communicate with dances and sounds. So, let's take this innate language and use it to our advantage. The arts can be a powerful learning tool and are a lot easier to integrate into a lesson than one may think.

Whoa! Whoa! Whoa," you may be thinking. "But I can't even draw a stick person. I can't dance to save my life. And sing... hah...that's funny. How can I ever incorporate arts into my lessons?" My first piece of advice is to keep it simple. Offer a child that hates writing but loves reading comics a chance to create his own superhero scene. Or pull out a MadLibs book for the child struggling with parts of speech, have them illustrate or act out the final story. And that kid that is always drumming their pencils on the desk that can't quite get his multiplication facts, let them make a rap or dance to share with their classmates.

A second piece of advice...let students' voices be heard. The voice that speaks through misdirected behavior. That misdirected energy is your key to a treasure trove of magic. It's a cryptic message saying, "help me...I don't know how to say this in words." The chronic fidgeter who is in love with space may need to turn their desk into a rocket ship control center, or the painfully shy child with a stutter who finds refuge in singing may lead the class in a morning song.

Yes, I hear ya…I don't have that much time to cater to every child individually on top of the 50 million other things I must do. Let's not reinvent the wheel. Find resources that are already out there. Hit up the library. Reach out to your arts colleagues (I guarantee they are chock full of ideas).
And most importantly and possibly the easiest…ask the kiddos!!! They have the answers. Find out what they are into, what shows they like, what apps they use, what foods they enjoy, and what music they listen to. They want to be heard. They want to know they are valued. And they have a wealth of information just waiting to be shared.

So now let's say you have your lessons in front of you, and they are ready to go, but you are uncertain how to put the arts into them. A simple solution is to offer an arts activity as a final project option. Instead of a 10-page paper, scale it to 5 plus a drawing/song/performance. Another strategy is to put mini activities layered within teaching blocks. After 10 minutes of learning about frogs, pull up a YouTube video on how to draw frogs for kids, and let them create and possibly list three facts they just learned on the back. After the next 10 minutes, play a game of leap frog, and after every hop the students share a fact. Another strategy is to work backwards. Think of or find a creative project you'd like to do and build your lesson around it. Say you saw this awesome hot air balloon craft on Pinterest. Maybe it could relate to science and how hot air rises, or English and the book 'Around the World in 80 Days,' or math and calculate volume and area. The possibilities are endless…you're only limited by your own imagination.

In the classroom, you will have learners of all abilities…some will catch on lickety-split while others may take a few detours before finding the "aha highway." Regardless, they all speak the language of the arts. Some will gravitate towards music, some will be into acting, while others will find drawing more their thing. The key is to let their interests guide the creativity so they can speak in the innate language they are fluent in.

When we allow all of our students to leverage their interests to learn, two amazing things happen: one that we have students that move from disengaged to engaged, and the other, that we learn so much more about our students and their interests. Encouraging student choice and voice increases engagement for everyone and can allow children who don't typically feel comfortable in the classroom setting, such as our ADHDers, to blossom.

Inviting and encouraging students to share their diverse talents takes inviting student choice and voice one powerful step further. When we celebrate children's talents and showcase them, we accept them and celebrate them. Our deepest purpose in education is to bring kids closer to their own purpose, and by inviting children to develop their diverse talents, we are inviting all children to realize their potential, including our ADHDers who are so vulnerable to being underserved.

Specific Benefits to Children with ADHD

Engagement, positive mindset, achievement

REFLECTION POINTS

Let's continue this conversation and learn from one another. Share your thoughts in a tweet with the hashtag #ADHDGlobalConvo and feel free to mention me directly @BiscottiNicole.

- How can I encourage students to share about their talents?
- How can these talents be included in our classroom to support the standards taught?
- How can our classroom become a place that celebrates students' diverse talents?

TEACHER'S TOOLBOX: SUBJECT SPECIFIC ADHD ACCOMMODATIONS FOR ALL

In the previous chapter, we explored whole-class interventions that are general to almost all classrooms. In this chapter, we'll discuss strategies that are more targeted to specific subject areas. There is, of course, considerable cross over skills between disciplines. For example, if you teach Science, learning reading strategies is relevant. Additionally, the structure of classrooms is as diverse as the teacher's imagination, so it's possible that you may find a way to modify or incorporate these strategies differently. Please share your classroom strategies on Twitter with the hashtag #ADHDGlobalConvo.

Technology and Gamification

"I like to play video games because you can focus on them because they're interesting and there's always something else to do like a challenge. Also I can pick which challenges I want and do things that are on my level. I think learning should be fun and sometimes have games involved to challenge us."

Most parents worry about the amount of "screen time" that their kids are getting daily. Our students are connected and tech-savvy; in many cases, they have been driving their content since they were toddlers. Technology and gaming are very engaging, offering personalization, instant feedback, and almost infinite opportunities for differentiation. For many children, it is their preferred format for learning.

Scott Nunes, Educator, Edtech Coach, and Podcast Host, offers practical strategies that leverage the elements of technology and gaming that are attractive to students. His suggested approach is not a push for kids to spend more time in front of the screen but rather incorporates elements of technology that attract kids to increase classroom engagement. These strategies are excellent for all students and, with their focus on engagement, provide support specific to the challenges of the ADHD learner.

> Students need constructive ways to engage material, be themselves, and need the space to engage their superpower! I am also a big fan of the SIOP method and strategies, particularly the I do, we do, and I do form of teaching a lesson. By giving students with ADHD hope and the tools needed to not only survive, but to thrive in a school environment, we as educators are empowering them to become the best version of themselves. One way that I have engaged these types of learners, it's through gamification in conjunction with project-based learning, game-based learning, and short bursts of explicit direct instruction.
>
> What is great about gamification is that learning becomes a game. I have taken design and constructive elements from

games and added them into my classroom structure. Students can level up in a variety of ways. Student choice is embedded in many of the assignments. I utilize Choose Your Own Adventure models, choice boards, and EDU Protocols to provide structure and differentiation.

Rather than assign schoolwork, I make missions available to my students. I offer support in the form of dynamic lessons with video support hosted on my school's LMS, Schoology. I have an attractive folder system, with a folder just for self-guided help organized by topic. This allows students to access and navigate the materials after I have delivered instruction at their own convenience and own pace. Also, within these missions, students have the opportunity for side quests. The side quests are great because they reinforce the learning, are low-risk, formative, and engaging. An example of a side quest I commonly do is a digital or physical break out. This activity is similar to the concept of an escape room. Students are given clues to break out by solving a series of problems/scenarios infused with academic challenges.

This can look like students reading a short passage and organizing key elements of that passage and then using those key elements to unlock a physical lock, which will grant them access to a box that has the next clue/task. By the time they reach the end, they will have gone through a few iterations of this. Not only is it fun, but it is a great way to infuse cross-curricular items, soft skills, and higher-order thinking. I find that my ADHD students, in particular, are quite gifted at this type of academic challenge, and they tend to be the leaders when we do this type of challenge as a group.

I thoroughly enjoy highlighting how my students, like those with ADHD, have essential leadership skills. Their superpower enables many of them to take the lead when given the opportunity, but that doesn't mean that they have to be leaders all the time, or that their value is dependent upon their leadership skills. Many of them are also great ideators, creators, and craftspeople, and we need more people like this! One thing that the COVID-19 pandemic of 2020 has shown me is that we need people who are highly adaptable, can think outside the box, and come up with solutions to fluidic challenges.

Part of gamification is that the learning opportunities can always be scaled up or down, and they are differentiated so as to have a grand appeal and applicability. This adaptability is crucial in reaching all learners and making my content accessible to them. Plus, it extends the opportunity to showcase their learning in different modalities. That doesn't mean as an English teacher that I stopped teaching how to write essays or that we stop writing essays altogether. We actually do more writing and do more argumentative discourse supported with analysis. I achieved this by chunking things into smaller bits. Rather than writing one large essay, we work on developing topic sentences one day, and then we'll do introductory paragraphs another day, or focus solely on thesis statements.

I utilize digital tools such as Nearpod (an interactive digital presentation tool) to constructively gauge where my students are at, give them practice, teach, and reteach a series of standards. By using this tool, I'm able to quickly give everyone a voice, offer up individualized support when needed, highlight learning, and embed game elements. What this would look like is I give a quick 8-10 minute lesson with examples and non-examples on what a proper topic sentence looks like. I then show a series of short clips from a familiar film, like Harry Potter. After each clip students will share a topic sentence, I will make them all anonymous, and then constructively provide feedback on a number of the responses. With each succession, there is a gradual release of responsibility. The first one I will model, then the second students in small groups will generate a shared response, followed by a small series of individual responses. I will often incorporate sentence frames or sentence starters when introducing a new item; I will gradually remove those supports.

Simultaneously, students will vote using the like feature, and whoever gets the most likes gets additional XP. Now, this isn't a popularity contest, we're strictly merit-based, and I will vary the conditions for voting. Sometimes it will be to select the worst example of a topic sentence or the funniest topic sentence. I may even ask for the shortest, most succinct topic sentence or the most elaborate and elongated, yet grammatically correct topic sentence. I may even have them submit their topic sentence in the form of a meme (they love this one!) Make sure you have embedded digital citizenship constructs before trying this one, though.

Children are dynamic, energetic, and learn through play. Adding elements of gamification in the classroom, such as designing assignments as missions and providing choices, creates excitement about learning. Chunking assignments supports organization and focus while offering multiple ways to give and receive feedback encourages community and taking responsibility for one's learning.

. . .

Specific Benefits to Children with ADHD

Engagement, movement, focus, organization

REFLECTION POINTS

Let's continue this conversation and learn from one another. Share your thoughts in a tweet with the hashtag #ADHDGlobalConvo and feel free to mention me directly @BiscottiNicole.

- How can I design assignments to be perceived by students as challenges?
- How can I incorporate gaming elements into my instruction?
- What technology can be integrated into my classroom instruction to support the needs of different learners?

Math

"I don't like when teachers explain a lot of steps in math. It helps when the steps are simple so I can focus more. Usually I know the answer but I don't know how to explain how I did it in my head and write it down."

Math, which requires focus, organizational skills, and remembering steps, can be tough for kids with ADHD. Jason loves math but performs terribly in this subject at school. A major pitfall for math success is confidence. Even though Jason feels good about his ability to do math, he is not confident about his ability to achieve in school, which is the single largest factor in positive outcomes in math. Jason, or even children with ADHD, are not the only students that share this challenge. Children's math performance is positively correlated to their level of confidence academically (Supriadi, 2020).

Alice Aspinall, Math Teacher and Author, describes a whole class approach to math that not only incorporates movement for all children, but reframes math as a natural part of the environment rather than an isolated academic discipline. She offers practical suggestions for coaching students to show their work in ways that are natural and accessible to them while addressing the organizational support that many students need to navigate multiple steps in math problems. Proactively embedding movement and accommodating for common struggles in math is an effective way to reduce anxiety and increase achievement.

The mantra, "Good for all, necessary for some" (Ontario Ministry of Education, 2004, p. 44), serves as a reminder that good practices can assist all learners. I am offering ideas to assist with learning mathematics centering around movement, solving long problems, and explaining your thinking.

All students can benefit from movement throughout the day. Hands-on learning is effective and fun for students, and mathematics can easily be taught interactively—both in the classroom and at home. One way to teach math through movement is by combining concepts with sports or fitness. There is a lot of math involved in athletic activities, and children love when they can merge the two areas. A multitude of mathematical concepts can be incorporated into physical activities—these are not restricted to team sports. Here are some general ideas to help facilitate planning. Use different activities to practice math concepts whenever possible. Remember that math is all around us.

- bike riding – rates, circumference;
- hopscotch – counting, skip counting, algorithms;
- jump rope – counting, skip counting, rates;
- scored games – counting, skip counting, basic operations;
- track and field – time, counting, rates, measurement.

When students struggle with problems that involve a lot of steps for solving, I recommend a checklist. Create a simple checklist with success criteria and keep it in sight while working on a problem. Make sure the steps are in point-form and not very wordy—this is for two reasons: so that the student is not overwhelmed with information and to serve as a memory aid while not giving away the entire step. Refer to the list as you work through each step and check off the step when done to trigger moving on to the next step. The more you use your checklist, the less you will need it as you become more comfortable with the problem.

Many students have trouble showing or explaining their thinking when solving a math problem. The response I often hear from students is that they just know the answer in their head and do not know how to put their thinking down on paper. When this happens, I suggest trying two approaches. First, I ask the student to just tell me verbally how they got to the answer. If the student can articulate this, then I ask them to write exactly what they said—no need to worry about math statements, or spelling or grammar, just write the words. If the student has trouble verbalizing their thought process, then I pose a different question: choose a younger child that you know; how would you tell this young child how you got to your answer? This approach often helps them find an explanation because it disrupts the notion that their teacher wants an advanced or complicated explanation.

All of these strategies might be especially useful for children with ADHD, but they are not specific to any learner. These strategies are beneficial to all children when learning mathematics.

The methods for embedding math standards into the larger classroom are endless and obviously highly dependent on the particular standard being taught. When we move math from an isolated discipline into everyday life, we reduce the anxiety around math. Adding specific organizational strategies is an important piece and supports all learners.

Specific Benefits to Children with ADHD

Organization, completing tasks, engagement

REFLECTION POINTS

Let's continue this conversation and learn from one another. Share your thoughts in a tweet with the hashtag #ADHDGlobalConvo and feel free to mention me directly @BiscottiNicole.

1. How can I use my students' interests as a part of math lessons?
2. What are ways that movement can be incorporated into lesson design?
3. How can I embed organization strategies of steps into lessons?

Reading

Literacy is a fundamental academic skill that many students struggle with. We know that to be successful learners, our students have to be successful readers. Children with ADHD can have specific challenges with reading due to their hyperactivity and difficulty focusing. When we meet these learning challenges effectively, we have an opportunity to increase engagement for all learners. Laura Robb, teacher, author, and educational consultant, shares her personal perspective as a child with ADHD developing her reading skills.

>I am hyperactive and most likely ADHD, but when I was in elementary school, the behavior had not been named. My grandmother Annie described me as 'not being born with enough sitting cells!' However, her love for me transformed

into understanding, and she allowed me to move while talking to her and walk around the kitchen and dining room in the middle of dinner. I believe she sensed that these impulses to move were beyond my control.

In the primary grades, I received punishments for wiggling in my chair and moving it around as if the chair was my dance partner. Daily, teachers called me out for not attending and staying on task, for continually falling off my chair, and for impulsively leaving my seat and walking to the window. I can still recall the strong urge to look outside and see trees and people.

In second grade, I remember my mom begging me to follow the rules. I couldn't find the words to explain why that wasn't possible and only said, "I can't" which resulted in a time out —a punishment that was torture for me. Those two words, "I can't," summed up my daily challenges—something deep inside of me, something I couldn't control, caused me to walk and run and lose focus.

My behavior embarrassed and perplexed my parents, who stopped taking me to the movies because after sitting for five minutes, my impulse to move took hold, and I'd be walking up and down the aisles. Soon, the manager would receive complaints and invite my parents to remove me. Two hours of sitting felt like an eternity to me. My brother, four years older, always sat, listened, followed directions, and stayed on task. I was the family's anomaly—no one could figure out the why behind my behavior and actions.

During years of teaching, my struggles with impulsive

behavior helped me understand children who couldn't sit still or attend. There was fourth grade Ethan, who could focus better when I let him stand at his desk, feet tap-tapping while he wrote in a journal or discussed a book with peers. Adam, a wonderful reader and writer in my eighth grade English class, walked around the room most of the period. Before collaborative discussions, he'd scoop up the basketball in the back corner of our classroom. For several minutes Adam would run and dribble the ball in the hallway and then return to class, able to concentrate. Fifth grade Jake nearly overturned the kidney-shaped reading table by bobbing his legs up and down. When Jake and I meet, he smiles widely as I tell him that he can stand during the reading group. Other group members forget that Jake's hands and feet are in perpetual motion as soon as the book we're reading and discussing grabs their attention.

These students have one thing in common with me: when we find a book that speaks to us, we can sit and read for twenty to thirty minutes. True, feet are always moving and body wiggling, but we could attend to the story.

In college, when I had breaks between some classes, I could release some of my energy by walking or jogging around campus. Now, while I'm writing this piece on my computer, my feet are tapping, I'm wiggling around in my chair, and swiveling it left-to-right. As an adult, I've accepted that part of me has to be in motion. I've also learned that I need to get up and move around more frequently than others do, especially when I have to concentrate.

So my message to teachers everywhere is to accommodate

students who have ADHD. Take the time to talk to ADHD students. Find out what works for them. Give them choices and let them decide when they need to move and release energy. Others won't be distracted if you're not.

Think out-of-the-box and know that sameness in a classroom environment and how students complete a task does not have to be the norm. By empathizing with students' impulsive behavior and helping them cope with it, you strengthen their social-emotional well-being, enable them to learn, and set the stage for a time in their lives when they will develop ways to tap into their creativity, collaborate, learn, and be productive members of their communities.

Being a responsive educator is the foundation for any successful classroom strategy. When we approach all students with an open heart and mind, we can observe what their specific needs are. When I reflect on my love of reading, I realize that it centers around my desire to learn about things that are interesting to me. Reading offers an infinite possibility of the expression *student choice and voice.* Wherever possible, give students the choice of reading material, topic, and level of complexity. Inspire a love of reading by allowing them to find what "fits" them. Opportunities for movement such as performing skits and even stories rather than only reading them are an exciting way to engage students who need movement. Using a visible timer and allowing for stretching or wiggle breaks helps with both motivation and permitting movement. Whole-class strategies like teaching guided note-taking, establishing reading goals, and creating written or drawn summaries support focus and organization in young readers.

TYPICAL REASONS
Why Kids Don't Like to Read

EXCUSES	SOLUTIONS
Reading is Boring	Choose 3 books you think you might like to read. One of them usually turns out to be really good.
Reading Takes too Long	Read along with an audio book. Doing this will improve reading speed and fluency.
The Book is Way too Long	Choose books that have more pictures or chunk them, read a chapter at a time.
I Hate Reading 'Out Loud'	Record your oral reading privately and then read along with it. You will see your mistakes and your confidence will improve.
I Don't Understand What I Read	Go over new vocabulary before reading. Try to make an association with the new word with something you already know.

scholarwithin.com

© 2020 Scholar Within, Inc. Printed with permission

Specific Benefits to Children with ADHD

Engagement, movement, organization

REFLECTION POINTS

Let's continue this conversation and learn from one another. Share your thoughts in a tweet with the hashtag #ADHDGlobalConvo and feel free to mention me directly @BiscottiNicole.

- What interventions can I use for either my whole class or groups in my class to support more engaged readers?
- How can I allow for kids' need to move while reading?
- What resources can I leverage to expand students' ability to choose reading that interests them?

I NEED TO MOVE! – LIVING WITH HYPERACTIVITY

WHAT IT FEELS LIKE TO HAVE HYPERACTIVITY

"Let me explain something to you about moving: I have to move. I feel like my body is going to explode if I don't move almost all the time unless I'm calm but most of the time I just have to keep moving."

Not all kids who are hyper have ADHD and not all kids with ADHD are hyper. Some have a presentation of inattentiveness rather than hyperactivity/impulsiveness which is sometimes referred to as ADD. For those who are hyperactive, it has a major impact on their ability to be successful socially and academically.

"Most of the reason that I get in trouble is because I need to move like all of the time. I'm either in trouble for actually moving or getting in trouble because I'm being bad because I'm frustrated because I can't move. I know it's weird to like most people but I get super mad when I can't move."

My preferred approach is always to introduce interventions and supports that address children's' needs, both with and without ADHD. Whether children are hyperactive or not, they are all served by increased movement in the learning environment. Traditional school has children sitting for hours on end with only very infrequent breaks for movement. Unfortunately, the amount of recess keeps decreasing in most schools as well. This is all happening as we see a rise in obesity and aggression.

INCORPORATING FREQUENT MOVEMENT REDUCES CHALLENGING BEHAVIOR

> *Increased physical activity during the school day can help children's attention, classroom behavior, and achievement test scores. Meanwhile, the decline of play is closely linked to ADHD; behavioral problems; and stunted social, cognitive, and creative development."*
>
> — DARELL HAMMOND

Dr. Brad Johnson, author of *Learning on their Feet,* discusses the benefits of movement that is incorporated into whole class activities along with providing ways for incorporating movement.

> Physical activity improves brain plasticity, which allows children to learn more easily. Second, there is evidence that contact with the natural environment has a calming effect on children. And third, exercise releases endorphins (neurotransmitters that produce a feeling of wellbeing), which makes chil-

dren feel more relaxed. Finally, the brain processes movement in the same part of the brain that processes learning. So, if students are sitting still then the learning process is actually hindered, rather than enhanced.

Several studies provide evidence that many years of fine motor exercise allows brain reorganization and nerve growth. Physical movement such as standing, stretching, walking or marching can help the brain focus better. For instance, if students feel drowsy, they should be allowed to stand at the back of the room for up to two minutes and stretch on their own. I remember when I taught middle grades science; I would always have the students moving.

Even when taking notes, I would let the students stand by their desks, sit on the floor, or even lie on the floor. If a student had too much energy, I would let them go to the back of the class and do push-ups. Students quickly adapt to these situations, so there are very few behavior issues because this becomes the norm for the classroom. The change in levels and body positions help develop the vestibular system (inner ear and balance), change blood chemistry, as well as develop core muscles.

Physical activity, especially core strength and balance, helps develop the same part of the brain where learning is processed, called executive functioning. Executive functioning includes cognition, organization, focus, working memory, emotion regulation and the ability to multitask. These are all the things that help students focus, stay on task, behave properly, and succeed academically!

KINESTHETIC LEARNING STRATEGIES

"I am listening to you when I'm moving. I can listen and I can multi-task but I have to keep moving. I know that moving is distracting. Sometimes it's better if I sit by myself or like in an area that's not touching the other kids so I don't bother them but I have to keep moving."

Students' need for learning can be addressed by chunking activities into sections of time with breaks for movement interwoven to facilitate increased focus. Sometimes teachers will ask students to read a page and then do jumping jacks or stretch and continue. The possibilities for chunking learning activities and incorporating movement breaks are endless. I have found that it's fun to decide on these as a class and to use students' suggestions.

"I would love for my teachers to make learning more fun and like a game that we can all move around together in and still learn stuff. I was thinking that the teacher could use a ball, not like a hard one, but one that we can all catch like a bouncy ball. The teacher could throw the ball to a student and the student would have to answer a question. If they get the answer right they could throw it to someone else and they could also ask a different question. If someone gets an answer wrong then they could give the ball to someone near them to have a try. I think this would be fun to practice facts and math problems, maybe even for reading comprehension about a story. I think fun things like this where I could move would help me to focus and not have to move around the classroom so much. I like moving and throwing and any physical activity."

Kinesthetic learning refers to lessons that are designed to merge movement and learning. These learning opportunities offer students the experience of learning by doing. They incorporate movement and are project-based. For many kids, this creates relevancy and is a key aspect of increasing their engagement with the content. These types of lessons tend to stay with us since they are not just times when we received knowledge but also *experienced* something. I do not remember any of my second-grade science class. I know that we studied plants at some point, but I cannot tell you a single thing that I learned during any lessons other than the time that we spent planting our seedlings and watching them blossom. Similarly, I do not recall reading about the Roaring 1920s, but I do remember all of the information that I gathered to create a magazine from the time period. These examples from my own childhood are not memories of lessons; they are memories of experiences that I learned from.

9 Activities for Kinesthetic Learning

1. Use letter tiles
Activities that use letter tiles are some of the most effective activities for teaching reading and spelling.

2. Get outside
Trace letters, words, or phonograms in the sand or dirt. Is it winter? Go outside and stomp giant letters in the snow.

3. Ooey-gooey fun
Fill a zip-top baggie with shaving cream, whipped cream, soap, glue, or pudding. Seal and write letters on the bag!

4. Bounce around
Spell words while jumping on a trampoline, bouncing a ball, or playing catch. Yell out one letter for every jump, bounce, or toss!

5. Get crafty
Use playdough, pipe cleaners, or Wikki Stix to form letters and words.

6. Play hopscotch
Write letters or words in each square of a hopscotch grid. When your child picks up his marker, have him read the letter or word in the square.

7. Use a beach ball
Write letters or words on a beach ball. Have your child throw the ball in the air, catch it, and say the letters or words closest to his thumb.

8. Have a "snowball" fight
Use ping pong balls, Nerf balls, or crumpled paper as snowballs. Write letters or words on index cards and tape them to the wall. As you call out letters or words, your child must find them and throw snowballs at them.

9. Play hide and seek
Write words and sentences on pieces of paper and hide them around the room. When your child finds a piece of paper, he must read it before searching for the next one.

Want more? Find 10 more activities on our blog!
https://blog.allaboutlearningpress.com/19-activities-for-kinesthetic-learning

blog.AllAboutLearningPress.com

(c) 2020 All About Learning Press, Inc. Reproduced with permission.

PERMISSION TO MOVE

"I don't like when teachers tell you to sit still all of the time, because as you know, I'm bad at sitting still and then I kind of automatically end up in trouble. I like it better when they give me an option to move around. One teacher that I had actually put tape on the floor around my desk in like a box shape. She let me move however I wanted to inside the box. The funny thing to me is that no one else was allowed to step in my box so it gave me a comfortable vibe. I felt like I could move all that I wanted and not get in trouble for bothering anyone else and no one could bother me either."

As a parent, I really did not like the tape around Jason's area intervention. I honestly felt like my child was being physically labeled; however, he loved it. Having a designated area made him feel like he could move, and it also made him feel secure in his own space. The next year another teacher tried the tape box intervention, but it flopped because that teacher did not enforce others staying out of the box. What I learned through this is how important it is for Jason to have permission to move and to know that he won't get in trouble for doing so. When other children went into his box, he no longer felt that he could move freely. He apparently did not mind having a marked space because that space afforded him the freedom to move at will.

Allowing Jason to move and planning for his need to move alleviates a great deal of tension for him, the teacher, and even the other children. Sometimes when Jason's energy is higher, he may need to leave the classroom or go for a short run. The best-case scenario is that Jason and the teacher discuss his need for movement and develop a proactive plan. Some teachers have given him a card to hold up when he needs to leave the classroom, while others have asked that he directly request permission.

"I like to get out of the class and run so it's fun for me to do errands for the teacher. I mean I know I can't really run in school but it just feels good to get out and I like to help the teacher. Sometimes my teachers let me bring books and stuff like that to the library or the office. I think it helps me focus to do that when I have more energy some days."

"I don't like when teachers touch me when I'm mad because it makes me feel even more mad. Sometimes it does help me if I'm really, really comfortable with the teacher or if it's like my mom but usually it makes it worse. It makes me feel awkward and also kind of trapped and like if I move more I will make them mad."

In my own classroom, I have found that partnering up with kids in this way has helped me to meet their needs and to build rapport. My kids are in high school, so the constraints are a bit different than with younger children. I fondly remember one student who needed to move from time to time, so we agreed that he could leave quietly and walk around the portables for a few minutes when needed. Sometimes I would discreetly ask if he felt that he needed a walk when he was being disruptive. He was always much more on task when he would return. I know that this student tended to be disrespectful to other teachers, but he was always very kind and polite to me and even stopped by the following year a few times when he needed to speak with an adult on campus.

SAVE RECESS

"I don't like when I lose my recess because it makes me even more mad and frustrated. Recess is the only option that I had to do something and move around and then it's just gone."

I have had numerous disagreements and debates with different teachers that Jason has had over his recess. Taking away recess from a hyperactive kid is a really counterintuitive and ineffective strategy. My first concern when teachers want to take away his recess is that it will cause an escalation of challenging behavior from him because when he can't release his energy, he becomes angry. When you consider that hyperactivity is a symptom of their neurological condition, it becomes questionable if this is even a fair punishment. There are numerous alternatives in terms of punitive measures to taking recess away, many of which yield better results. I worry that Jason will end up in more trouble and question whether that is fair since we know that he requires movement. When we are not responsive to children's needs, we damage our relationship with them.

Besides depriving children of their need for movement, taking recess away as a punishment can make it harder for us to arrive at the underlying need for support, going back to form versus function. Jason's behavior during math at one point was that he was distracted, unfocused, and did not complete his assignments. Jason's view was that the assignments were mostly worksheets and that he couldn't sit still and concentrate on them. He would then often get up, distract others, and find other creative ways to be disruptive. Rather than examining the function of Jason's behaviors and addressing the support that he needed, his recess was taken away so that he could complete the worksheets during that time. He did not ever complete the worksheets during recess; he became increasingly frustrated and angry and then disruptive. This would prompt him to receive an even bigger consequence, which usually resulted in removal from the classroom. The common thread here is that his need for movement was never recognized and met. He became increasingly angry, continued to escalate his misbehavior, and then faced growing consequences up to removal (rejection) from the learning environment. I really wish that I were describing an isolated incident or that Jason was the only kid that this ever happened to.

It can be tricky and awkward to approach educators as a teacher-mom. It must be similar to how chefs feel when they go out to eat. It was always very clear to me why taking recess away never worked, even though I also understood why it made sense to teachers to take away fun time to complete his work. We have a responsibility to structure our support offered and consequences in a way that *teaches* children.

REFLECTION POINTS

Let's continue this conversation and learn from one another. Share your thoughts in a tweet with the hashtag #ADHDGlobalConvo and feel free to mention me directly @BiscottiNicole.

- What support for kids' need to move is built into my classroom procedures?
- What are ways that I encourage movement as a part of learning?
- Which kinesthetic learning strategies work best for my class?

MAKING FRIENDS - SUPPORTING ALL STUDENTS IN INCLUSION

POINTS TO PONDER

- What is meaningful inclusion?
- How can we prepare children to deal with the challenging behaviors associated with ADHD?
- How do children benefit from making friends with ADHDers?
- What are whole classroom strategies that support meaningful inclusion?

∼

MEANINGFUL INCLUSION FOR ALL

Education policies and legislation implemented the inclusion model in schools, but meaningful inclusion doesn't exist without thoughtful planning and support for all. Although children with special needs are increasingly taught in the "least restrictive environment," they are not often reaping the social and academic benefits that the model offers. Meaningful inclusion is a model in which children are able to create and maintain friends with children of diverse perspectives. At its best, inclusion offers the opportunity to advance society by developing social competencies in childhood. At its worst, it throws children together without any support and results in the reinforcement of stigmas and an increase in feelings of isolation.

According to a study by Wilens and Spencer (2010), "Attention-deficit/hyperactivity disorder (ADHD) is among the most common neurobehavioral disorders presenting for treatment in children and adolescents. ADHD is often chronic with prominent symptoms and impairment spanning into adulthood" (p. 1). ADHD may be a common disorder, but it is invisible. There are no physical characteristics of children with ADHD that can be seen without doing a scan of their brain activity. Essentially, ADHD is an invisible disability. When children frequently interrupt others, get angry quickly, and have sudden impulses, those around them are not always able to understand that they are working within the parameters of a very real neurodevelopmental disorder.

Meaningful Inclusion allows children to learn not only from the teacher but from one another. They learn to value diverse perspectives and talents. Children also learn to successfully navigate friendships, even with children who think differently than themselves. Meaningful inclusion does not happen without adults providing children with support as they confront the challenges of developing socially and emotionally with their peers. Although the benefits are enormous, meaningful inclusion requires careful planning from responsive educators.

. . .

Bridging Understanding

The conventional wisdom is currently that inclusion is supported by systemic, school-wide practices such as restorative justice, Positive Behavior Intervention Support (PBIS), and trauma-informed school practices. While these components do support inclusion, they do not address one very obvious missing piece. How does the child sitting next to a kid who cannot sit still, does not follow social cues, and talks incessantly interact with this child? We can focus on compassionate education, and we should, but that does not specifically bridge understanding between these two children.

Before a child plays with my son, they are better off understanding that he is hyperactive and quick to anger. As a child themselves, they are probably not equipped to identify those behaviors, separate them as behavior that is frequent for Jason (not take it personally), and then respond positively. I can't even do that consistently, in all honesty. Jason has twin sisters that are fifteen months older than him. I often observe how they react to him since they are children themselves but have considerable experience relating to Jason. I have noticed that they tend to call him out on his explosive and hyperactive behavior and then either distance themselves or compensate for him, depending on the situation, and probably mostly on their own mood and the level of sibling tension present at the moment. The girls will often say something like, "Jason, you always yell when you get mad." This is generally followed by an eye roll and walking away, or by one of his sisters deciding to accommodate him to lessen his frustration. The ideal moments are when the girls are able to identify the behavior, the reason, and then either distance themselves for their own well-being or talk him through calming down.

I recall an incident that changed my perspective. For years I thought that Jason had the full responsibility of understanding that his behavior was often not "socially acceptable" and that he must adapt or be isolated. This seemed to be the harsh reality until one day when I realized that a more compassionate and accepting option is available. The Inclusion Model is powerful, not only for the child with a disability, but for all students. It is an opportunity for us to become more accepting of all members of society and to gain experience in honoring differences and learning to collaborate and share with others, which ultimately provides us with important social skills as well as an enhanced perspective.

As I was wrapping up my own school day, I saw a missed call from Jason's school, which I returned. I was told that Jason and another boy had hit each other and that because of that, Jason would receive a consequence at school. This part was not surprising to me, in all honesty. The administrator went on to describe the words that they used when speaking to Jason and explained that "other kids don't want to play with him because he hits a lot and makes a lot of noise" and that "he has to understand that kids don't like his behavior and don't want to be around him." I felt that I couldn't argue with her logic as I held back tears and quickly got off the phone.

Another teacher near me overheard the conversation. She said that she was shocked that this was the best the school could do for Jason. She expressed outrage that they were resigning themselves to Jason being unsuccessful socially since he obviously could not self-regulate at this point due to a disability. I actually defended the school's position and said, "What can they do about it? It's true, other kids don't want to deal with his temper, nor should they have to." She replied that her son has Down's Syndrome and that no one would ever call her and tell her that other kids didn't want to play with him, much less tell her son that directly. She went on to suggest that the school could handle Jason's behavior difficulties as an opportunity for understanding just as they do with her son or with a child that has a physical disability.

That day was a real turning point for me in my understanding of inclusion and the implications that it can have for all children. Implemented correctly, educators have the power to create a more accepting society.

Before we can have a positive impact on society and promote acceptance, as educators, we have to look inward. Are we more likely to enthusiastically include a student whose disability is physical rather than behavioral? According to a study done by Jeremy Monsen in 2012, this is, unfortunately, the case. He showed that teachers are more likely to willingly provide inclusion to students without behavioral issues. Maybe this is because, on some level, we do not fully accept that the concept of a behavioral disability exists. I know that I personally had a tendency to think that all kids had equal control over their behavior. Being Jason's mom has taught me how far off the mark I was.

SUPPORTING CHILDREN WHO DON'T HAVE ADHD

Children who have to interact with peers with ADHD are often placed in very stressful situations. We must work to both protect the child with ADHD from social isolation as well as provide the student interacting with them with tools and knowledge to avoid negative outcomes for them as well. I learned a lot about strategies to support children that don't have disabilities from a conversation with a very wise first-grader, Ameerah. Her teacher took a few very insightful steps to support meaningful inclusion in her classroom:

Use the buddy system and make sure that pairings support both children.

Ameerah shared, "I didn't really know my friend, and then one day my teacher went up to me, and she asked if I wanted to be his friend and take care of him. I didn't really know what she meant, but I said, 'ok.' Now we're friends, and we play together a lot."

Prepare kids for challenging behavior by ensuring their safety, and helping them to understand that outbursts are not personal and the result of impulsivity, not their friend's personality.

"Sometimes he gets on Godzilla mode and gets really mad, and sometimes he throws chairs and hits people. When he gets on Godzilla mode, I try to calm him down, and sometimes I can, but usually he needs Miss. B. to help him. When he gets on Godzilla mode, I know he's not mad at me; he's just mad. He's really kind when he's not on Godzilla mode, and I know he'll always be my friend when he's done being mad. Sometimes I do get scared that he could hit me with a chair or something. When he gets really bad, I can tell a grown-up if he needs Miss B."

Be open and honest about differentiated discipline and the purposes that it serves.

"If he does five good things in a day, he gets cookies and gets to go with Miss B. Sometimes she gives me cookies because I help him. I don't get mad that he gets cookies and the other kids understand it also because our teacher told us that everyone learns in different ways. Miss B. helps him to calm down."

. . .

Be open and honest about everyone's needs and limitations.

"When the other kids don't want to be his friend and play with him, he gets more frustrated and madder. Now since my teacher explained to us how he gets mad easily and learns differently, people started wanting to be his friend, and he has more friends, and now he's happy and calms down more. He wants to be happy with everyone."

A thoughtful approach to fostering meaningful inclusion for all has lifelong benefits for every child in the classroom community.

> I think it's really great that my teacher explains things to the class because it's gonna be easier if there's someone I don't know, and I already know how to be friends with people who have ADHD."
>
> — *AMEERAH RUIZ-WILEY, 7 YEARS OLD, FIRST GRADER*

Ameerah comforting her friend

PRE-GAME STRATEGIES: WHERE SEL MEETS ADHD

Any investment of time spent embedding Social Emotional Learning into classroom culture has a huge return for all children. There are many elements and strategies of SEL that are supportive for all students while addressing specific typical ADHD behaviors. When Jason was in preschool, the program that he was in thankfully emphasized early Social Emotional Learning skills (SEL). Jason is now in fourth grade, and I have seen how this foundational piece has served him through the years. Specifically, I can tell you that the following strategies have stayed with him:

Labeling and Identifying Ways to Express Emotions

In the chaos of emotions that little ADHDers tend to experience, learning to recognize and to label their emotions is crucial. This skill also lays the foundation for enhanced empathy and social skills since a logical next step is to begin to be able to recognize emotions in others. I remember that in the preschool, there were several faces showing different emotions with labels to cue the children in identifying the emotion that they were feeling. Jason almost always chose the face labeled "frustrated," except that he used to awkwardly skip the first "r" and insert a "k" in the first syllable giving us all a chuckle. One day I was upset, and I remember three-year-old Jason hugging me and saying that it was ok for me to be "frustrated" (the way he pronounced it, of course).

After labeling emotions, it becomes important to talk about ways that emotions can be expressed. We all have the power to decide how we want to express an emotion. Teaching children that they have the ability to manage emotions rather than emotions running them is powerful. Learning to assign supportive expressions to our emotions is arguably a lifelong pursuit. As an adult, this can look like me feeling sad and choosing to take a walk over a movie and a pint of ice cream. As a child, this might be feeling mad and going to play with someone else rather than hitting the kid you're playing with.

A powerful strategy for teaching about identifying emotions and discussing ways to express them is through reading material. Stories teach us, inspire us, and are arguably the oldest form of teaching and learning. Stories are a non-threatening way to present emotional awareness concepts without singling any child out while providing entertainment as well. Perhaps that is why storytelling has been such a key part of learning for humans for millennia.

Melissa Thorpe Sidebotham, principal and author of *Oof! and The Big Feelings*, shares,

> Reading books about identifying and understanding emotions can be one way to be proactive with your students or your own children. It also provides a touch-point for when Big Feelings take over. It doesn't make it about the child and their inability to cope; it makes it about their ability to recognize the signs their body is giving off. The opportunity is then there to step outside of the feeling and begin to regain some control. It can also help them to realize that they are not alone when they have a storybook character to identify with.

Illustrations by Noella Bickel, adapted from the characters in "Oof! and the Big Emotions" by Melissa Thorpe Sidebotham

The faces with labels and reading stories work well in a classroom for younger children, but there are other ways that the same concept can be adapted for older children. Teachers can use visual cues such as posters, vocabulary walls of emotions that kids can add to, discussions, the list is endless. Teachers can also model labeling emotions when speaking with students. If you have a great strategy for teaching labeling emotions, please share it on Twitter with the hashtag #ADHDGlobalConvo.

Creating a Space between Anger and Action

The impulsivity of ADHD is particularly tough when you're a kid and may not even fully realize that it's not in your best interest to act without thinking. The SEL program at Jason's preschool emphasized support with self-regulation by allowing kids to ask to sit alone or to express that they needed help calming down. I learned from their example and began to actively seek strategies to help Jason to cool down when he became angry. We have tried many strategies, including breathing exercises, counting, journaling, private conversations, having designated objects he can throw or slam, agreeing to a time out and then to talk when he's ready, and letting him go to his room and scream. Some of these would not work in a classroom; however, the main components that seem to be necessary are lowering the stimulation level, support from an adult, creating a pause, and a safe way to release energy.

Jason is a child who benefits from the opportunity to retreat into his own space. That probably should have been apparent to me as a mother when someone gave him a play tent for Christmas, and he was very territorial about not allowing his sisters in the tent where he would play for long periods. At the time, I dismissed it as a pretty normal reaction to having twin sisters that are only fifteen months older. Over the years, this behavior has taken different forms, but he still often seeks the refuge of a quiet place with less stimulation, particularly when he's feeling upset.

When Jason went to preschool, his teacher was wise enough to provide Jason with a designated space to decompress when needed. Sometimes he would create a fort and be allowed to sit in it when he needed to. In elementary school, some teachers have allowed Jason to go to the back of the room when he preferred to be alone. Many teachers have begun to integrate a quiet area that is accessible to any student in the classroom, a smart and proactive whole class intervention.

Melissa Thorpe Sidebotham shares,

"Here are some things I have found helpful to have in my teacher's classrooms for children to use for self-regulation.

- A designated spot for all students to retreat when they need space. It can be a separate table or desk or a spot on a rug. Some students find it comforting to be able to be under something, so sitting under this desk can be allowed.
- A liquid motion bubbler, glitter calm-down jar, or snow globe
- Stress balls from very soft to more difficult to squeeze (more resistance)
- A newborn baby brush for calming sensory input on arms
- Foam roller for pressure on large muscle groups like the thighs
- A weighted lap pad for some compression (a weighted blanket is not as realistic in a classroom setting)
- Stiff putty to pull on or dig small plastic toys out of with fingers
- Noise-canceling headphones to lessen auditory stimulation

All of these items can be stored in a storage box in the designated area. I have found that all students appreciate having the option to take some space. The ones who need it the most will feel better about using it, and it also provides an opportunity for the teacher to model when they are frustrated too."

Providing opportunities for children to have a quiet place to be and other tools for self-regulation classroom-wide is an important and proactive way to support children's social-emotional learning. When we provide children classroom supports, we are partnering up with them rather than allowing them to fail and then punishing them.

Mindfulness

There are many different methods and programs to introduce universal self-regulation support. An increasingly popular strategy is mindfulness. Shilpi Mahajan, Author and Founder of *Fablefy*, discusses whole-class strategies that benefit everyone while specifically meeting the needs of children with ADHD who struggle with hyperactivity, self-regulation, and social skills.

> Mindfulness, in its simplistic terms, is, 'Paying attention to the present moment experience, with curiosity, without judgment, and with compassion.' While clinical psychology is yet to reach a complete operational definition of Mindfulness, two components are clear (a) orienting one's attention purposefully to the present moment and (b) approaching one's experience in the present moment with curiosity, openness, and acceptance.
>
> Initially introduced by Jon Kabat Jin for chronic pain, Mindfulness has found its way into various mental health conditions, such as eating disorders, anxiety disorders, depression, and substance use. Mindfulness enhances Prefrontal cortex functioning, which controls focus and executive function. It also increases release of dopamine, a neurotransmitter that is lesser in ADHD brains.
>
> Multiple studies have shown the effectiveness of Mindfulness training on children with ADHD. Mindfulness, when practiced, was able to increase attention and reduce hyperactivity in ADHD brains. Multiple findings in child and adolescent

samples are promising and demonstrate that mindfulness meditation training in the ADHD population is feasible and acceptable.

The great thing about Mindfulness is that it can be done anytime and anywhere. Educators who bring Mindfulness to the classroom will do a great service to all the kids. Kids have excess energy, and Mindfulness helps them regulate this energy in a positive manner. For kids with ADHD, this energy is even more difficult to harness. If educators and schools create a moment of pause, they will help the entire classroom in being effective and improve the overall class environment and culture.

Students with ADHD are often told that they are aggressive and disruptive. Children often don't want to play with them. Introducing a daily Mindfulness practice can create regulation in them and create a compassionate setup where educators can help support them. It can validate them and help them create a connection with their peers and teachers.

5 Easy Mindfulness practices for children that parents can do anytime are as follows:

1. **Buddy Breathing:** Allow kids to sit back to back by randomly picking partners. Let them sit and ask them to synchronize their breathing with each other. Allow them to take this moment of pause. Add a loving kindness activity to this process where kids can send loving kindness feelings to themselves and to the partner they are sitting with. A practice like this not only creates stillness but also creates compassion and connection.

2. **Mindful Walking:** A mindful walk can help delve a child's pent up energy while bringing movement during the day. Allow the kids to walk slowly around the classroom. Let them walk slowly and ask them to feel how their feet touch the ground. Continue this for 5 minutes, and after the Mindful walk, do a spidey sense exercise with a 5-4-3-2-1 focus. 5 things that can be seen, 4 things that can be heard, 3 things that can be touched, 2 things that can be smelled, and one thing that can be tasted
3. **Mindful Relaxation:** A Mindful Relaxation helps children engage with their sensations and different parts of their bodies. Allow them to feel their sensations by tightening and relaxing different parts of the body. Start with the feet and move to the head. You can use guided meditations available on YouTube.
4. **Sitting Still Like A Frog:** Sitting Still Like A Frog is another excellent activity to alternate movement with stillness. Based on a famous book by Eline Snel, Sitting Still Like a Frog engages little children. Pretend the classroom is a pond, and children are jumping from one lily pad to the other like frogs. After 10 jumps, pretend they are sitting still on their favorite lily pad as they wait for their bugs. Ask them to be still for a count of 10.
5. **Candle Breaths:** Children can pretend they have a candle in front of them. Ask them to do a controlled breathing activity where, as they exhale, the candle flame flickers away from them, and as they inhale, it comes towards them. The breath has to be so slow, so as to not allow the flame to extinguish.

Teachers who help their classrooms with Mindfulness-based meditation empower the child's agency, make them self-aware, and create connections within the classroom. Mindfulness helps create a space where kids dispel their excess energy and are able to focus better.

REFLECTION POINTS

Let's continue this conversation and learn from one another. Share your thoughts in a tweet with the hashtag #ADHDGlobalConvo and feel free to mention me directly @BiscottiNicole.

- How can I have Meaningful Inclusion in my classroom?
- How can I best support my students without ADHD?
- What whole class accommodations will best support my students?

THE ADHD VILLAGE

How can I create a powerful partnership with parents? Who is on my team to support my students with ADHD? Who can I speak with when I need support with accommodating the needs of my students with ADHD?

A PARENTS' PERSPECTIVE

Supporting children with special needs requires effort from every adult involved. Children's needs evolve as they grow, and what worked at one time may not work at all at another. There is not a solution, a cure, or a magic classroom intervention that is going to bring great success and academic gains overnight...although we may really wish there was. This is a long-term effort involving frequent communication, trial and error, adjustments, flexibility, and commitment. The communication between parents and teachers becomes even more crucial.

Before educators even begin to think about establishing a working relationship with parents, I believe that it is essential to try to understand their perspective. When I begin to think about how I can convey what it has felt like for me, I'm almost at a loss for words. The range of intense emotions that I have felt over the years is almost impossible for me, the writer, to convey. I will do my best to paint a picture, however, because I firmly believe that the essential first step is to begin to understand the parent's perspective. Please keep in mind that this has been my experience and, of course, is not representative of every parent. My sharing of my experience can never replace the insight gained from listening to parents with an open heart.

My first son was pretty close to being the most compliant child ever. When he went to school, he completed his homework and always had good grades. He did get in trouble once in the second grade for rolling his eyes during a lesson, but he dutifully wrote an apology letter to the teacher. He is currently in a training program to become an officer in the United States Marines, which requires adherence to high standards. *I raised a very compliant young man.*

Nicholas didn't qualify for the ROTC scholarship on early admission because his fitness scores were too low. He was told he had three weeks to improve them. He focused on his fitness, and when he returned to the committee, he had the highest scores in the state that year by a pretty good margin. *I raised a remarkably focused young man.*

I knew that Nicholas's success had a lot to do with his diligence and focus and the fact that compliance wasn't difficult for him. Imagine my dismay when my next son entered preschool, and I began to receive daily phone calls from the school about incidents of him running away, throwing things, displaying violent outbursts, etc. *The ability to comply with rules and focus that had come so easily to one son completely eluded the other.*

Even worse, nothing I did or said would make him stop. I tried everything and spent hours pleading with Jason to "just behave." He would tell me that he wanted to be good but then hang his head and say that sometimes he couldn't make himself calm down. *It would take me years to understand that my little boy had been clearly telling me what the "problem" was all along.*

At the writing of this book, Jason is in the fourth grade, and I still feel afraid, intimidated, worried, embarrassed, and frustrated a lot of the time about Jason's education. When I see the school on my caller ID, I know that 99.9% of the time, they are calling me because they need help calming Jason. I think it would be fair to say that all parents feel intense distress when their children are in distress. I know that Jason's acting out and meltdowns are hard on staff and even students around him. I feel terrible about that, but I also know that when Jason is at that point, an intervention either failed to happen or failed to work as we predicted it would. I feel that we are failing to adequately support him, and underneath it all, I'm concerned about my child's future.

When a teacher calls a parent of a child with ADHD, trust me, theirs is not the first phone call. The parents already know that their child is not focused and compliant in class, and this has probably been concerning them for a while. Most people have more than one child, and the parent you're calling might be very good at raising children with those admirable traits. I was, but when it came to Jason, I didn't know what to do. Neither my experience as a mother, nor my master's degree in education, nor having been a teacher prepared me to support Jason in being successful in school. *Like many other parents of children with ADHD, I was scared for my child's future and felt helpless and ashamed of his behavior.*

Educators have an opportunity to have a long-lasting impact by opening a dialogue about how to provide support and to scaffold academic skills. Parents are looking for "solutions". They also have valuable knowledge about their child's interests, likes/dislikes, experiences, etc. Investing time in creating a strong working relationship with parents leads to collaboration and discussions about options for supporting the child. *When parents and educators come together, the child now has a team of the adults closest to them in their corner.*

A powerful next step is asking children for their input. Children want to succeed and to please their parents and teachers. My younger son felt very badly about not being able to measure up to his brother's conduct in school. He received a lot of negative feedback and messages from adults in his life for his inability to be compliant and focus. We can view this struggle as an opportunity to begin teaching self-advocacy skills. They know better than anyone what they're feeling and where they need support. *We can learn from children with ADHD when we start to ask questions.*

Students become our greatest teachers if we listen. As interesting as we think our lessons can be, a student might be throwing pencils every day during a writing lesson because they really struggle to focus, which causes them to feel overwhelmed. *What if our ADHDers can show us new ways of teaching and learning that raise engagement and achievement for everyone?*

When we begin to have conversations that are collaborative and empowering rather than punitive, we stop negatively affecting the self-efficacy of parents and the self-esteem of children. Instead of excluding a child and a parent's insights by making assumptions about them, we have the choice to listen. Rather than calling them with a list of complaints, consider discussing observations and asking them to collaborate with you. *Listening with an open heart and mind is the first step in implementing meaningful support.*

It's hard to hear impatience, annoyance, or blaming in the tone or words from the adult on the phone. I do understand exasperation at times, because I have shared that emotion, but the others hurt as a parent. They hurt deeply, and if I were to be honest, they terrify me because my deepest fear is that you will give up on my kid. They also frustrate me because if I can hear those emotions, then Jason has been sensing them in the events that led to the phone call. In these moments, I'm worried about his feelings and likely to become defensive because I know that Jason is likely to react badly when he senses negativity from adults. From my conversations with other special needs parents, I feel that I can speak for the majority when I say that we are more worried about our child being successful than any educator probably can imagine. These are our babies, and we know they're not always easy to educate, but we need your help.

THE TEAM MEMBERS

As I complete this book, it occurs to me that as someone that just wrote a book about ADHD, I continue to be both a parent and educator that struggles to support children with ADHD. ADHD is a humbling condition because of its complexity that requires us to continuously seek to understand and continue learning. Luckily, this is a team effort. Not only do educators and teachers support one another, but we also have other team members to rely on.

Parents

Sometimes the best way to figure out which intervention will be most successful is to speak with a child's parent. They have the benefit of having seen how their child reacts to different environments and approaches over time. As a parent, I can tell you that a few times, I tried to explain that a particular approach would end badly but was ignored. I honestly felt resentment when Jason was punished because he misbehaved in a situation that I tried to proactively warn about. I don't have all of the answers, but I know my child pretty well, and I felt that if I had been "heard," an unpleasant situation could have been avoided.

As educators, we don't have all of the answers, and it's more than ok to ask parents for their insights— it's wise. Some parents are hesitant to share their thoughts with teachers because they don't want to feel that they are overstepping or appear intrusive. An open and honest dialogue with parents can be the start of an effective collaboration that benefits everyone. Also, when a great working relationship is established, parents and teachers can work together closely to support kids in specific areas using a consistent approach.

School Counselors

Schools offer a variety of services and support on campus through the dedication of school counselors. They provide a continuum of support and interventions that varies from school to school. Jason has formed very close and supportive relationships with different counselors. They are usually the person that he speaks to when he is not able to be in the classroom because of disruptive or unsafe behavior. I have appreciated the effort spent by counselors in developing strong and trusting relationships with Jason. Additionally, Jason has benefited from small groups such as anger management with his peers. Through these group interventions, counselors are able to provide training in skills and coping mechanisms that children with ADHD need to thrive in school.

Counselors also provide support for teachers in many forms, including education about ADHD and help with working with specific children. Partnering up with counselors has helped me quite a bit over the years. I have learned a lot from them about ADHD and by understanding the support that they are giving kids. As a teacher, I often patterned my classroom interventions from what the counselors were doing to provide consistency.

Medical Professionals

ADHD is a neurological condition making medical professionals best able to understand children's limitations from a clinical perspective. Through their explanations of the functions of the brain and how it relates to learning and behavior, we can better understand the limitations faced by children with ADHD. The medical field offers several layers of support for children and families such as pediatricians, including those specializing in behavior and development, psychiatrists, psychologists, and counselors. The medical community offers multiple supports for ADHD, including counseling, both individual or family, and classes to learn more about the condition and how best to manage its symptoms. Increasingly doctors and teachers are working together and sharing information through seminars, reading material, and collaborative conversations.

SPREAD THE WORD

The biggest obstacle that kids with ADHD are facing is ignorance. It is a sad irony that ADHD is so common yet so misunderstood. Jason has been discriminated against and bullied verbally by teachers, family members, and other children. I don't believe that any of these people meant to harm Jason's self-esteem or to provide the direct opposite of a supportive learning environment. I think that the problem is that although we have come so far technologically, as a global society, we still have a very primitive understanding of mental health disorders. We have yet to adequately address inequities in education and meaningful inclusion in the classroom. How can we teach children to be inclusive if we are not inclusive? How can we provide support to our children with ADHD if much of our population does not even understand ADHD? These issues do not exist in a vacuum in education; they reflect a larger problem in society.

Clinicians do not spend a significant amount of time with their patients, and since ADHD is not a visible condition, they largely rely on parents and teachers to refer children for evaluations. If most of the population, including educators, do not understand ADHD, how can we assume that this is happening with any degree of consistency? Teachers and parents are the front lines in identifying children who may have ADHD.

We have to begin to normalize conversation about WHY children behave the way that they do. There is always a WHY and an underlying need waiting to be addressed. When we begin to view behavior in this way, we can positively impact children's lives. In considering the following scenario, we see the drastic difference in the type of impact that, as educators, we can have on children every day. In both scenarios, there was an impact; however, one was negative and the other positive. We cannot afford to continue to approach children's behavior from a lens of "right" and "wrong" without considering "WHY." The stakes are too high for kids.

Behavior: Jason constantly moves during instruction.	
Teacher's approach	**Potential Impact on Jason**
The teacher repeatedly calls him out and eventually loses their patience.	Low self-esteem, damage to the teacher-student relationship
The teacher speaks with Jason after class and they come up with a plan for Jason to be allowed to use a fidget object during the lesson and they agree that Jason will be allowed a water break after the lesson.	The opportunity for him to succeed academically, a better understanding of his own needs, increased self advocacy skills, a positive teacher-student relationship.

The change from punishment and marginalizing to identifying and supporting children with ADHD begins in many places. It begins with states mandating that teachers have training and education in special needs that is appropriate to the population of children that they teach under Inclusion. It begins with teacher education programs taking the initiative to adequately prepare new teachers to meet the needs of their students with special needs. It begins with district initiatives. It begins with advocacy. These are all large-scale initiatives, but supporting children with ADHD also begins with each one of us.

Children with ADHD reaching their potential begins with observing and asking questions with an open mind and an even more open heart.

LET'S BRING THE #ADHDGLOBALCONVO TO YOUR SCHOOL!

Visit nicolebiscotti.com and contact me directly to talk about your school's needs and how we can work together to better support your ADHD learners.

- Keynote Addresses & Talks
- Custom-Designed Workshops (Virtual & On-Site)
- Flexible Webinars

Every school engagement is designed to create awareness of ADHD from diverse perspectives, equip teachers and staff with effective strategies, and above all, spark conversation and collaboration for the benefit of ADHD learners.

REFERENCES

A.D.H.D. Poem. (n.d.)- Earl's News & Views. http://liverseed.ca/d-h-d-poem/

Ali, A. (2018). Individualized Teacher-Child Relationship (ITCR) Strategy to Enhance Academic Performance of Children with Attention Deficit Hyperactivity Disorder (ADHD). Journal of Educational Sciences & Research, 5(2), 37–44.

Ali, Z. (2019, January 2). ADHD in girls: Symptoms, early warning signs, and complications. Retrieved September 28, 2020, from https://www.medicalnewstoday.com/articles/315009

REFERENCES

Blum, K., Chen, A. L., Braverman, E. R., Comings, D. E., Chen, T. J., Arcuri, V., Blum, S. H. ...Oscar-Berman, M. (2008). Attention-deficit-hyperactivity disorder and reward deficiency syndrome. Neuropsychiatric disease and treatment, *4(5)*, 893–918. https://doi.org/10.2147/ndt.s2627

Bray, B. (2018, September 9) Spectrum of Voice Comment end: Developing Self-Regulation, Autonomy, and Agency. Retrieved November 29, 2020 https://barbarabray.net/2018/09/09/spectrum-of-voice-developing-self-regulation-autonomy-and-agency/

Catani, M., & Mazzarello, P. (2019). Leonardo da Vinci: A genius driven to distraction. Brain. Vasari G. Delle Vite De' Piu` Eccellenti Pittori Scultori Et Architettori. Firenze: Giunti; 1568. Translated by Gaston Du C. de Vere. New York: Alfred A. Knopp; 1996.

Center for Disease Control and Prevention. (2020). Research on ADHD. Retrieved September 28, 2020, from http://www.cdc.gov/ncbddd/adhd/research.html

Chang, Z., Lichtenstein, P., Halldner, L., D'Onofrio, B., Serlachius, E., Fazel, S. ... & Larsson, H. (2014). Stimulant ADHD medication and risk for substance abuse. Journal of child psychology and psychiatry, and allied disciplines, *55(8)*, 878–885.

Cordier, R., Vilaysack, B., Doma, K., Wilkes-Gillan, S., & Speyer, R. (2018). *Peer Inclusion in Interventions for Children with ADHD: A Systematic Review and Meta-Analysis.* BioMed research international, 2018, 7693479.

Crum, K. I., Waschbusch, D. A., & Willoughby, M. T. (2016). *Callous-unemotional traits, behavior disorders, and the student–teacher relationship in elementary school students.* Journal of Emotional & Behavioral Disorders, *24(1)*, 16.

de Ruiter, J. A., Poorthuis, A. M. G., & Koomen, H. M. Y. (2019). *Relevant classroom events for teachers: A study of student characteristics, student behaviors, and associated teacher emotions. Teaching and Teacher Education, 86.* https://doi.org/10.1016/j.tate.2019.102899

Einziger, T., Levi, L., Zilberman-Hayun, Y., Auerbach, J. G., Atzaba-Poria, N., Arbelle, S., & Berger, A. (2018). *Predicting ADHD symptoms in adolescence from early childhood temperament traits. Journal of Abnormal Child Psychology, 46(2), 265-276.*

Ghanizadeh A. (2011). *Sensory processing problems in children with ADHD, a systematic review. Psychiatry investigation, 8(2), 89–94.* https://doi.org/10.4306/pi.2011.8.2.89

Ginsberg, Y., Quintero, J., Anand, E., Casillas, M., & Upadhyaya, H. P. (2014). Underdiagnosis of attention-deficit/hyperactivity disorder in adult patients: A review of the literature. *The primary care companion for CNS disorders, 16(3)*, PCC.13r01600. https://doi.org/10.4088/PCC.13r01600

Gintner, G. G., & Mooney, P. (2015). Attention to ADHD: DSM-5 Changes, practice guideline updates and implications for schools. *Beyond Behavior, 24(2)*, 20–29.

Granot, D. (2016). Socioemotional and behavioural adaptation of students with disabilities: The significance of teacher–student attachment-like relationships. *Emotional & Behavioural Difficulties, 21(4)*, 416–432.

Gwernan-Jones, R., Moore, D. A., Cooper, P., Russell, A. E., Richardson, M., Rogers, M., ... Garside, R. (2016). A systematic review and synthesis of qualitative research: the influence of school context on symptoms of attention deficit hyperactivity disorder. *Emotional & Behavioural Difficulties, 21(1)*, 83–100.

Hamre B.K., Pianta R.C., Downer J.T., Hamigaki A., Mashburn A.J., Jones S., Brackett M.A. Teaching through interactions—Testing a developmental framework for understanding teacher effectiveness in over 4,000 U.S. early childhood and elementary classrooms. Elementary School Journal in press.

Heritage, M. (2018). Assessment for learning as support for student self-regulation. Australian Educational Researcher, *45(1), 51-63.*

Kendall, L. (2016). "The teacher said I'm thick!" Experiences of children with Attention Deficit Hyperactivity Disorder within a school setting. Support for Learning, 31(2), 122–137.

Lawrence, K., Estrada, R. D., & McCormick, J. (2017). Teachers' experiences with and perceptions of students with attention deficit/hyperactivity disorder. Journal of Pediatric Nursing, 36, 141–148.

Learning Disabilities Association of America, (2020). ADHD. Retrieved September 28, 2020, from https://ldaamerica.org/disabilities/adhd/

Ministry of Education. (2007). Differentiated instruction teacher's guide: Getting to the core of teaching and learning. Toronto: Queen's Printer for Ontario.

REFERENCES

Monsen, J., Ewing, D., & Kwoka, M. (2014). Teachers' attitudes towards inclusion, perceived adequacy of support and classroom learning environment. *Learning Environments Research, 17*(1), 113–126.

Moore, D. A., Russell, A. E., Arnell, S., & Ford, T. J. (2017). Educators' experiences of managing students with ADHD: A qualitative study. *Child: Care, Health & Development, 43*(4), 489–498.

Moore, D. A., Gwernan-Jones, R., Richardson, M., Racey, D., Rogers, M., Stein, K., Garside, R. (2016). The experiences of and attitudes toward non-pharmacological interventions for attention-deficit/hyperactivity disorder used in school settings: a systematic review and synthesis of qualitative research. *Emotional & Behavioural Difficulties, 21*(1), 61–82.

Parekh, R. (2017). *What is ADHD?* Retrieved September 23, 2020, from https://www.psychiatry.org/patients-families/adhd/what-is-adhd

Pilkey, D. (2020). *Meet Dav Pilkey.* Retrieved September 23, 2020, from https://pilkey.com/author

Porter, E. (2019). *What is hyperfocus and how does it affect kids and adults?* Retrieved September 28, 2020, from https://www.healthline.com/health/adhd/adhd-symptoms-hyperfocus

Proulx-Schirduan, V., Campbell, B., Case, K. I., & Shearer, C. B. (2009). Mindful education for ADHD students: Differentiating curriculum and instruction using multiple intelligences. *London: Continuum.*

Rief, S. F. (2012). *How to reach and teach children with ADD / ADHD: Practical techniques, strategies, and interventions. Germany: Wiley.*

Rock, Marcia L.; Gregg, Madeleine; Ellis, Edwin; Gable, Robert A. (2008-01-01). *"REACH: A Framework for Differentiating Classroom Instruction" (PDF). Preventing School Failure: Alternative Education for Children and Youth. 52 (2),31–47.*

Rogers, M., Bélanger-Lejars, V., Toste, J. R. , & Heath, N. L. (2015). *Mismatched: ADHD symptomatology and the teacher–student relationship. Emotional & Behavioural Difficulties, 20(4), 333–348.*

Sansosti, F. J., Cimera, R. E.., Koch, L. C. , & Rumrill, P. (2017). *Strategies for ensuring positive transition for individuals with attention-deficit/hyperactivity disorder. Journal of Vocational Rehabilitation, 47(2), 149–157.*

Sheridan, S. M., & Wheeler, L. A. . (2017). *Building Strong Family–School Partnerships: Transitioning from Basic Findings to Possible Practices. Family Relations, 66(4), 670–683.*

REFERENCES

Supriadi, S. (2020). *Pre-service elementary teachers: Analysis of the disposition of mathematical modeling in ethno mathematics learning* Elementary Education Online, Vol. 19, 2020

Tomlinson, Carol Ann (2004). *Point/counterpoint.* Roeper Review. 26 (4): 188–189.

Vygotsky, L. S. (1962). *Thought and language.* Cambridge, MA: MIT Press.

Wilens, T. E., & Spencer, T. J. (2010). *Understanding attention-deficit/hyperactivity disorder from childhood to adulthood.* Postgraduate Medicine, 122(5), 97–109. https://doi.org/10.3810/pgm.2010.09.2206

Williford, A. P., Maier, M. F., Downer, J. T., Pianta, R. C., & Howes, C. (2013). Understanding how children's engagement and teachers' interactions combine to predict school readiness. Journal of applied developmental psychology, 34(6), 299–309.

Young, A., Andrews, C., Hayes, C., & Valdez, C. (2018). Should Teachers Learn How to Formally Assess Behavior? Three Educators' Perspectives. Education, 138(4), 291.

CONTRIBUTING AUTHORS

Alice Aspinall, B Math (Hons), B Ed., Secondary Math Educator and Author of children's books, including *Everyone Can Learn Math* and *Look for the Math Around You*. www.everyonecanlearnmath.com

Barbara Bray, Creative Learning Strategist, Podcast Host, and Author of *Define Your WHY*. https://barbarabray.net

Peg Grafwallner, Instructional Coach, Author, Blogger, and National Presenter. Author of *Lessons Learned from the Special Education Classroom and Ready to Learn: The FRAME Model for Optimizing Student Success*. https://www.peggrafwallner.com/

Dr. Brad Johnson, Educator, Author, and National Speaker.

Dr. Kevin Leichtman, Educator, Director of Academic Mindset, and Author of *Teacher's Guide to the Mental Edge*

Kate Lindquist, M.Ed., Art Teacher

Shilpi Mahajan, Founder of Fablefy and Author. https://www.fablefy.com

Scott Nunes, Educator, Edtech Coach, and Podcast Host of Education Today and the TNT Edtech Podcast. www.scottnunes.net

Laura Robb, Teacher, Author, and Educational Consultant. https://lrobb.com

Melissa Thorpe Sidebotham, Educator, Co-Founder of The EDUTable, and Author

ABOUT THE AUTHOR

Nicole is a proud educator and mother who seeks to bridge understanding, spark conversations, and inspire through her teaching and writing. Our children are our greatest teachers, and writing with her son Jason has been an opportunity for reflection and learning.

Nicole is also the mother of Nicholas, Rose, and Julia. She has a Bachelor's Degree in Spanish from the University of Florida and a Master's Degree in Secondary Education from the University of Phoenix. At the time of the printing of this book, she is completing her second Master's Degree in Education Administration. She hopes to finish the doctoral degree in Education Leadership that she began someday—but there are other books waiting to be written first.

MY STORY OF WHY I BECAME A TEACHER

I do not come from a long line of teachers. I don't even come from a long line of educated people. My mother was the first person in my family to earn a college degree and I am the first to earn a Master's Degree in my family.

I do come from a long line of people who loved, valued, and believed in education though. Our values are transmitted in the smallest of actions. Maybe it's not always what we model as much as where we place our attention.

My father was a truck driver and never attended college but he taught me to value education. When I went to kindergarten, it was a huge deal. I received a new wardrobe called "school clothes" and I was not allowed to play in them! He made sure that I could write and do basic math before I even went to school so that I would be "ready." **School is an important place.**

When I had low grades, my dad fought tirelessly with the Dean to have me placed in advanced classes. At the end of the term when I did well, we sat in her office until she was available because he wanted her to know how well his daughter had done. **I can achieve.**

When I rushed through homework with poor penmanship, my dad made me write it over. When I cut school to hang out with friends in high school, he assured me that he could take time off of work and was happy to attend class with me. When I got a 97% on a math final, he told me that I was capable of 100%. **Learning is serious business.**

My mother taught me to value education as well. When my first grade teacher sent me a letter, my mother framed it and hung it up in my bedroom. **Teachers are important people.**

My mother spoke to me about social issues and read me thought-provoking pieces like Langston Hughes's words: "What happens to a dream deferred…" and Martin Luther King Jr.'s speech, "I Have a Dream…." She never told me to read, but I did because I watched her read all of the time. **Education gives you perspective.**

I saw my mother struggle to support us while she went to school for years. She worked nights so that she could attend college classes during the day. I watched her improve her financial status when she became a nurse. **Education opens doors.**

My grandparents taught me to value education through their stories. My grandmother grew up in poverty and thought that her only way out was by working multiple jobs. She always told me that her only regret in life was not knowing what she could have become. My grandfather's aspirations of being a doctor died in his youth when he left college because he couldn't keep up with night school and his construction job. **Education makes dreams come true.**

I earned a Master's Degree in Education and began teaching high school as a single mother of four children at 38 years old. Becoming a teacher was not an easy path for me. I chose education because when I had the opportunity to start over I wanted to dedicate the rest of my working life to a cause that I cared about. It's never too late to connect with your purpose. **I have a deep respect for educators and I'm proud to be one. I believe that education opens doors to connect students with their purpose.**

www.ingramcontent.com/pod-product-compliance
Lightning Source LLC
Chambersburg PA
CBHW071414070526
44578CB00003B/578